GENESIS

MW00424483

0

Joseph
the Dreamer

A Guided Discovery for Groups and Individuals

Kevin and Louise Perrotta

LOYOLAPRESS.

CHICAGO

LOYOLAPRESS.

3441 N. Ashland Avenue
Chicago, Illinois 60657
(800) 621-1008
WWW.LOYOLABOOKS.ORG

Nihil Obstat
Reverend Robert L. Schoenstene, S.S.L.
Censor Deputatus
February 9, 2004

Imprimatur
Most Reverend Edwin M. Conway, D.D.
Vicar General
Archdiocese of Chicago
February 11, 2004

The *Nihil Obstat* and *Imprimatur* are official declarations that a book is free of doctrinal and moral error. No implication is contained therein that those who have granted the *Nihil Obstat* and *Imprimatur* agree with the content, opinions, or statements expressed. Nor do they assume any legal responsibility associated with publication.

The Scripture quotations contained herein are from the New Revised Standard Version Bible: Catholic Edition, copyright © 1993 and 1989 by the Division of Christian Education of the National Council of the Churches of Christ in the U.S.A. Used by permission. All rights reserved. Subheadings in Scripture quotations have been added by Kevin and Louise Perrotta.

The Greek text of St. John Chrysostom's comments on Joseph and Potiphar's wife (p. 33), from "Homily 62 on Genesis," may be found in Migne, ed. *Patrologiae Graecae* (Paris, 1860). An English translation is available in Robert C. Hill, trans., *Saint John Chrysostom: Homilies on Genesis*, pt. 3, The Fathers of the Church: A New Translation, vol. 87 (Washington, D.C.: Catholic University of America Press, 1992).

The statement by Julian of Norwich (p. 44) is taken from Robert Llewelyn, ed., and members of the Julian shrine, trans., Enfolded in Love: Daily Readings with Julian of Norwich (London: Darton, Longman and Todd, 1980).

The quotation from St. Bernard's homily on St. Joseph (p. 46) is taken from his *Homilies in Praise of the Blessed Virgin Mary,* Marie-Bernard Saïd, trans., Cistercian Fathers Series, vol. 18A (Kalamazoo, Mich.: Cistercian Publications, 1993), 28–29.

The comments by Claus Westermann on Genesis (p. 57) are taken from his book *Genesis 37–50* Continental Commentary, trans. John J. Scullion, (Minneapolis: Fortress Press, 2002), 74–75, 76–77, 108.

The Latin text of St. Patrick's *Confession* (p. 85) may be found in D. R. Howlett, trans. and ed., *The Book of Letters of Saint Patrick the Bishop: Liber Epistolarum Sancti Patricii Episcopi* (Portland, Ore.: Four Courts Press, 1994), translation by Kevin Perrotta. An English translation may be found in R. P. C. Hanson, *The Life and Writings of the Historical Saint Patrick* (New York: Seabury Press, 1983).

Interior design by Kay Hartmann/Communique Design
Illustration by Charise Mericle Harper

ISBN 0-8294-2008-8

Printed in the United States of America
04 05 06 07 08 09 10 Bang 10 9 8 7 6 5 4 3 2 1

Contents

4 *How to Use This Guide*

6 *A Story for Your Enjoyment*

12 **Week 1**
There Goes That Dreamer
Genesis 37

22 *Not for Sunday School*

24 **Week 2**
Not Your Boy Toy
Genesis 39

34 **Week 3**
Tell Me Your Dreams
Genesis 40–41

48 **Week 4**
Well, Look Who's Here
Genesis 42

58 *What's Joseph Up To?*

62 **Week 5**
Take Me Instead
Genesis 43–44

76 **Week 6**
I Am Your Brother
Genesis 45; 46:28–31

86 *Afterwords*

88 *What's the Story with Joseph's Dreams?*

92 *Suggestions for Bible Discussion Groups*

95 *Suggestions for Individuals*

96 *Resources*

How to Use This Guide

You might compare the Bible to a national park. The park is so large that you could spend months, even years, getting to know it. But a brief visit, if carefully planned, can be enjoyable and worthwhile. In a few hours you can drive through the park and pull over at a handful of sites. At each stop you can get out of the car, take a short trail through the woods, listen to the wind blowing through the trees, get a feel for the place.

In this booklet, we will read the main portion of the story of Joseph in Genesis 37–50. We will take a leisurely walk through the six readings, giving ourselves the opportunity to think carefully about what we are reading and what it means for our lives today. Joseph's life certainly gives us a great deal to reflect on.

This guide provides everything you need to explore the story of Joseph in six discussions—or to do a six-part exploration on your own. The introduction on page 6 will prepare you to get the most out of your reading. The weekly sections provide background and explanations that will help you grasp what this biblical narrative means for today. Equally important, each section supplies questions that will launch your group into fruitful discussion, helping you to both investigate the biblical text for yourself and learn from one another. If you're using the booklet by yourself, the questions will spur your personal reflection.

Each discussion is meant to be a *guided discovery*.

Guided. None of us is equipped to read the Bible without help. We read the Bible *for* ourselves but not *by* ourselves. Scripture was written to be understood and applied in the community of faith. So each week "A Guide to the Reading," drawing on the work of both modern biblical scholars and Christian writers of the past, supplies background and explanations. The guide will help you grasp the message of Genesis. Think of it as a friendly park ranger who points out noteworthy details and explains what you're looking at so you can appreciate things for yourself.

Discovery. The purpose is for *you* to interact with the biblical story. "Questions for Careful Reading" is a tool to help you dig into the text and examine it carefully. "Questions for Application" will help you consider what these words mean for your life here and now. Each week concludes with an "Approach to Prayer" section that helps you respond to God's word. Supplementary "Living Tradition" and "Saints in the Making" sections offer the thoughts and experiences of Christians past and present. By showing what the story of Joseph and its themes have meant to others, these sections will help you consider what they mean for you. At a couple of points, "Between Discussions" will explore some aspect of the story in more depth.

How long are the discussion sessions? We've assumed you will have about an hour and a half when you get together. If you have less time, you'll find that most of the elements can be shortened somewhat.

Is homework necessary? You will get the most out of your discussions if you read the weekly material and prepare your answers to the questions in advance of each meeting. If participants are not able to prepare, have someone read the "Guide to the Reading" sections aloud to the group at the points where they appear. (Be aware that the guide for Week 5 is longer than usual.)

What about leadership? If you happen to have a world-class biblical scholar in your group, by all means ask him or her to lead the discussions. In the absence of any professional Scripture scholars, or even accomplished amateur biblical scholars, you can still have a first-class Bible discussion. Choose two or three people to take turns as facilitators, and have everyone read "Suggestions for Bible Discussion Groups" (page 92) before beginning.

Does everyone need a guide? a Bible? Everyone in the group will need his or her own copy of this booklet. It contains the entire text of the readings from Genesis, so a Bible is not absolutely necessary—but each participant will find it useful to have one. Some of the questions call for reading passages of Scripture that are not included in this booklet. You should have at least one Bible on hand for your discussions (see page 96 for recommendations.)

How do we get started? Before you begin, take a look at the suggestions for Bible discussion groups (page 92) or individuals (page 95).

A Story for Your Enjoyment

Isn't it amazing how a good story can leap over canyons of time and space, bringing strangers near and making them seem familiar? You may never have met any sheep and goat herders who carry all their belongings around with them on donkeys. You may not know any family with twelve brothers and—simultaneously!—four mothers. Yet when a story about such a family begins "When [Joseph's] brothers saw that their father loved him more than all his brothers, they hated him, and could not speak peaceably to him"—well, it's easy to feel that this family is as close as the family next door, or closer. Hearing about a father's favoritism and brothers' envy, we immediately feel that we are on common ground with these people. We suspect that their story will involve conflict, tragedy, and, hopefully, reconciliation—as our own families' stories sometimes do.

Joseph and his family are far away from us. They lived thirty-three centuries ago or more in the dry hill country of Canaan (home of modern Israelis and Palestinians) and in the lush, marshy delta of the Nile River. Yet their experiences of longing for a parent's love, of maturing through suffering, of bearing the responsibility of compassion toward family members, of perceiving the hidden hand of God in human affairs—these themes play out in our own lives also.

Given its broad appeal, Joseph's story has been retold many times. Most prominent in recent years has been Tim Rice and Andrew Lloyd Webber's *Joseph and the Amazing Technicolor Dreamcoat.* For many of us, say "Joseph" and the songs of their musical begin playing in our heads. But the biblical story has its own unique character and flavor. It may be true, as the title of Rice and Webber's song proclaims, that "Any Dream Will Do" if you stick with it through thick and thin; in any case, however, that is not the message of the Joseph story in the Bible. You will enjoy the biblical story most if you silence the echoes of its later retellings and try to approach the original as though for the first time.

But is the account of Joseph indeed a *story* to be *enjoyed?*

To some, the word *story* indicates fiction. It might seem that calling the account of Joseph a story denies that it is historical. In the case of the account of Joseph, however, *history* and *fiction* are not an either-or.

On the historical side, Joseph and his family were links in a chain of actual people stretching from Abraham to Jesus. The account of Joseph (in the book of Genesis) provides the background to the account of the Israelites' departure from Egypt (in the book of Exodus) by explaining how they came to be in Egypt in the first place. Since there is a historical core to the Exodus account, there is at least a historical kernel to the Joseph account, too. On the fictional side, the account of Joseph is an imaginative blend of historical traditions and other material, composed in such a way as to instruct a much later generation of readers. In other words, it is composed as a good story. Thus the account of Joseph is history in the form of a story. This blending of historical and fictional elements was comfortable for people in the ancient Near East but is foreign to us, who expect our historians to keep fictional elements out of their history writing.

The blending of fiction with history in the account of Joseph does not make it any less true. Straight historical narratives are not the only kind of writing that communicates truth. Other kinds of writing—novels and poems, for example—can be true, even if they are not factual. Nor is the account of Joseph any less authentically God's word for not being written in the manner of modern history. When God inspired the biblical authors, they remained fully human authors. They wrote in their own languages, according to the outlook of their own cultures. The writings they produced belonged to their particular world as much as the clothes they made and the houses they built. Yet, by God's grace, their writings communicated his message not only for their times but for our time also.

It is possible to read the account of Joseph with an eye to its historical dimension, pausing at every step to consider the historical background and ask to what extent the events occurred as recounted. But such an approach is very complicated—so complicated that it would distract us from reading the account itself. Besides, even if we were to investigate all the conceivable historical questions, we would still ultimately come back to the story as it is written in order to ponder its meaning for us. In this guide, then, we will not have much to say about the historical character of the story, except to offer some information about the background that is useful for understanding it.

What about *enjoying* the story? Doesn't such an approach trivialize reading the Bible? After all, the Bible is something we are supposed to study, believe, and obey.

Well, of course, we take up the story of Joseph hoping for more than enjoyment. We hope to meet God in his word—a serious matter indeed. Yet the most direct path to this awesome encounter in the story of Joseph is, quite simply, to enjoy it.

Under God's inspiration, the human authors of Scripture produced a wide variety of writings. In order to hear God's voice in these writings, we need to tailor our reading to the particular purpose and form of each. If the writing is a theological argument, such as Paul's letter to the Galatians, we need to apply ourselves to understanding his reasoning. If the writing is poetry, we should appreciate its beauty. As St. Basil pointed out centuries ago, the psalms draw us into communication with God by the beauty of their music. If, as in the account of Joseph, the writing is a tale artfully told, we should enjoy it.

To enjoy Joseph's story, however, does not mean giving it a quick read and a smile. Enjoying the story means approaching it as we would a first-class novel, movie, or play: entering into it, identifying with the characters, probing their motives, evaluating their decisions. To enjoy the story involves examining the artistry of its construction and reflecting on parallels with our own experiences. If we enjoy the story of Joseph in this thoughtful way, we will discern its depth and wisdom. It will begin to live in our minds and hearts—thus becoming God's word in us.

If you read the story of Joseph with care and attention, questions will inevitably occur to you. For example, you may wonder whether Joseph bears some responsibility for his brothers' dislike for him. Do his dreams express his own desires or God's will? Does Joseph change in the course of the story, and if so, what causes the change? What motivates him to treat his brothers as he does? Where and how is God present in the story?

Perhaps surprisingly, it is not easy to give definitive answers to these questions. The narrator has described some of the situations in a way that leaves them open to more than one interpretation and has not given us enough information to determine which interpretation is correct. The basic story line of Joseph's life is clear enough. But the narrator has left gaps and ambiguities along the way.

These gaps and ambiguities stand as the narrator's invitations to explore the story carefully. "Consider alternative interpretations," he seems to be saying, "and reach your own conclusions." His purpose, it seems, is to lure us deeper and deeper into the story. In order to close the gaps and resolve the ambiguities, we reread and reread again. Characters who may have appeared two-dimensional at first reading, Joseph above all, gradually become more rounded. One scholar, Meir Sternberg, remarks that while the suspense of wondering how the story is going to turn out holds our attention only during our first reading, the gaps and ambiguities keep us interested long after we know the ending. In this guide, we will point out some of the intriguing gaps in the story and some of the clues that may help to bridge them.

It is worth noting that the narrator leaves not only gaps that produce ambiguity but also gaps that require us to exercise our imagination. He relates key incidents in vivid detail while passing over years of Joseph's life in Egypt without a word. He tells us what people say and do but leaves us to infer what they think and how they feel. He does not describe the terror of being kidnapped, the dispiritedness caused by chronic hunger, or the despair of indefinite imprisonment. He leaves it to us to fill in these blanks as best we can.

You will notice that we have been speaking of "the narrator." Who was he? Little can be said about him with certainty. He was a master storyteller; he belonged to the people of Israel. Almost certainly he did not complete the work alone; others added to it and revised it. When and where did he work? Possibly in

Jerusalem between the tenth and sixth centuries before Christ. (How's that for vague? It's like saying that the author of *Moby Dick* possibly lived in America between AD 1700 and 2200.) Fortunately, ignorance about the narrator's identity, situation, dates, and audience does not prevent us from enjoying his story.

A little background is helpful. Joseph's story reflects a period when Egypt is already a large, developed, and powerful nation, and Canaan is a land of small cities and towns inhabited mostly by shepherds and peasant farmers. Egypt has a strong central authority—the government of the king, called Pharaoh—with a system of administrative districts, food-storage facilities, and, of course, tax collections. This authoritarian system primarily benefits the small class of officials who run the government departments, army, and temples. But the system has advantages for the rest of the population, providing stability and buffering them from the most severe natural fluctuations, such as droughts, that spell disaster for their less highly organized neighbors in Canaan.

Joseph is born into a family of wandering shepherds who for some generations have experienced a relationship with the God who later reveals himself to Moses and ultimately makes himself fully present in Jesus of Nazareth. In earlier chapters of Genesis, God has promised Abraham, Abraham's son Isaac, and grandson Jacob that he will make their family great and will give them the land of Canaan. Joseph is one of Jacob's sons.

Some of God's communications with Joseph's great-grandfather, grandfather, and father occurred through dreams—not surprisingly, since people in the ancient Near East regarded dreams as a point of contact between the divine and human realms. In these dreams, as well as in other ways, God revealed himself directly to Joseph's forefathers—and to at least a couple of his foremothers. But Joseph's dreams are different from theirs. His dreams are more symbolic, and God does not directly reveal himself in them. Indeed, there is no record of God ever revealing himself to Joseph or speaking to him directly. This is an important feature of Joseph's life—and one that may make it easier for us to identify with him than with his ancestors.

Joseph is born into a family where parental favoritism has wrought conflict. Joseph's grandfather Isaac had favored his son Esau while grandmother Rebekah favored Esau's twin brother, Jacob. Seemingly in reaction to this treatment by his father, Jacob deceived his father into giving him the paternal blessing that should have gone to his brother. After this deception, Jacob had to flee Esau's wrath. He traveled to his family's relatives in an area in present-day southern Turkey, where he married his uncle's two daughters and also took two of their slave girls as his concubines. Between them, these four women bore a dozen sons and one daughter. Repeating the pattern of parental favoritism, Jacob preferred Joseph and Benjamin, the two sons of his favorite wife, Rachel. Although Joseph was not the first of Jacob's twelve sons— he was number eleven—Jacob treated him with the favor a father might have been expected to lavish on his firstborn, probably because Joseph was Rachel's firstborn. In fact, Jacob sometimes speaks as though Rachel were his *only* wife and her two sons his only children. When the story of Joseph begins, Rachel has already died giving birth to Benjamin.

Oh, one final piece of background information is important. A while before the story begins, the family was camping with their flocks near a town called Shechem (modern Nablus, a Palestinian city in the territory known as the West Bank). A young man of Shechem raped Jacob's daughter, Dinah, and then proposed marriage to her. In response, the brothers plotted revenge. They lulled the townspeople into thinking they agreed to the marriage proposal and were willing to make a treaty with the whole town. Then, when the Shechemites' guard was down, they sneaked into town and slaughtered all the men. This tells you something about the brothers Joseph has to deal with as his story begins.

THERE GOES THAT DREAMER

Questions to Begin

15 minutes
Use a question or two to get warmed up for the reading.

1 What's the nicest article of clothing you ever received when you were growing up? What's the most outrageous?

2 This question is for everyone who remembers being in a class that had an obvious teacher's pet: did the favoritism make you angry?
❏ No.
❏ Yes—at the pet.
❏ Yes—at the teacher.
❏ Yes—at both.
❏ Yes—at myself for not being the pet.
❏ No. I was the pet.

5 minutes
Read the passage aloud. Let individuals take turns reading sections.

The Reading: Genesis 37

A Tale of Love and Envy

2 This is the story of the family of Jacob.

Joseph, being seventeen years old, was shepherding the flock with his brothers; he was a helper to the sons of Bilhah and Zilpah, his father's wives; and Joseph brought a bad report of them to their father. 3 Now Israel loved Joseph more than any other of his children, because he was the son of his old age; and he had made him a long robe with sleeves. 4 But when his brothers saw that their father loved him more than all his brothers, they hated him, and could not speak peaceably to him.

5 Once Joseph had a dream, and when he told it to his brothers, they hated him even more. 6 He said to them, "Listen to this dream that I dreamed. 7 There we were, binding sheaves in the field. Suddenly my sheaf rose and stood upright; then your sheaves gathered around it, and bowed down to my sheaf." 8 His brothers said to him, "Are you indeed to reign over us? Are you indeed to have dominion over us?" So they hated him even more because of his dreams and his words.

9 He had another dream, and told it to his brothers, saying, "Look, I have had another dream: the sun, the moon, and eleven stars were bowing down to me." 10 But when he told it to his father and to his brothers, his father rebuked him, and said to him, "What kind of dream is this that you have had? Shall we indeed come, I and your mother and your brothers, and bow to the ground before you?" 11 So his brothers were jealous of him, but his father kept the matter in mind.

Conspiracies and Deception

12 Now his brothers went to pasture their father's flock near Shechem. 13 And Israel said to Joseph, "Are not your brothers pasturing the flock at Shechem? Come, I will send you to them." He answered, "Here I am." 14 So he said to him, "Go now, see if it is well with your brothers and with the flock; and bring word back to me." So he sent him from the valley of Hebron. . . .

17 . . . Joseph went after his brothers, and found them at Dothan. 18 They saw him from a distance, and before he came near to them, they conspired to kill him. 19 They said to one another, "Here

comes this dreamer. 20 Come now, let us kill him and throw him into one of the pits; then we shall say that a wild animal has devoured him, and we shall see what will become of his dreams." 21 But when Reuben heard it, he delivered him out of their hands, saying, "Let us not take his life." 22 Reuben said to them, "Shed no blood; throw him into this pit here in the wilderness, but lay no hand on him"—that he might rescue him out of their hand and restore him to his father. 23 So when Joseph came to his brothers, they stripped him of his robe, the long robe with sleeves that he wore; 24 and they took him and threw him into a pit. The pit was empty; there was no water in it.

25 Then they sat down to eat; and looking up they saw a caravan of Ishmaelites coming from Gilead, with their camels carrying gum, balm, and resin, on their way to carry it down to Egypt. 26 Then Judah said to his brothers, "What profit is it if we kill our brother and conceal his blood? 27 Come, let us sell him to the Ishmaelites, and not lay our hands on him, for he is our brother, our own flesh." And his brothers agreed. 28 When some Midianite traders passed by, they drew Joseph up, lifting him out of the pit, and sold him to the Ishmaelites for twenty pieces of silver. And they took Joseph to Egypt.

29 When Reuben returned to the pit and saw that Joseph was not in the pit, he tore his clothes. 30 He returned to his brothers, and said, "The boy is gone; and I, where can I turn?" 31 Then they took Joseph's robe, slaughtered a goat, and dipped the robe in the blood. 32 They had the long robe with sleeves taken to their father, and they said, "This we have found; see now whether it is your son's robe or not." 33 He recognized it, and said, "It is my son's robe! A wild animal has devoured him; Joseph is without doubt torn to pieces." 34 Then Jacob tore his garments, and put sackcloth on his loins, and mourned for his son many days. 35 All his sons and all his daughters sought to comfort him; but he refused to be comforted, and said, "No, I shall go down to Sheol to my son, mourning." Thus his father bewailed him. 36 Meanwhile the Midianites had sold him in Egypt to Potiphar, one of Pharaoh's officials, the captain of the guard.

Questions for Careful Reading

10 minutes
Choose questions according to your interest and time.

1 The narrator presents a family in crisis (37:2–11—unless noted, all biblical citations in this book refer to Genesis). Who is to blame? Support your answers with specific verses.

2 Why does Joseph tell his dreams? What does he think of them?

3 Many Scripture commentators— as well as Joseph's family members—find the dreams "obvious" and "self-explanatory." What do you think?

4 When do the brothers show solidarity? When do they disagree?

5 At this point, what is your impression of Joseph? Jacob? Reuben? Judah? of the brothers as a whole? Again, cite specific verses.

6 Do Joseph's dreams come from God or from himself? Is there any way to tell?

A Guide to the Reading

*If participants have not read this section already, read it aloud.
Otherwise go on to "Questions for Application."*

37:2–4. Disaster is brewing in Jacob's family, and this teasingly
open-ended introduction suggests that no one is blameless. In the
Hebrew, verse 2 alone abounds with seemingly deliberate ambiguities. Is Joseph an apprentice shepherd, caring for the sheep with
his brothers, or is he shepherding his *brothers,* in the sense of
lording it over them? Does he give his "bad report" about the
brothers once or regularly? Is Joseph a responsible lad or a
priggish squealer? Is he even truthful?

Jacob loved Rachel more than his three other wives, and
he favors her firstborn over his ten older sons. He proclaims his
favoritism by making Joseph a distinctive garment that all but
shouts, "I am Dad's *real* firstborn." It is safe to assume that this is
not just a nice gift. Scholar Claus Westermann observes: Jacob is
"raising the boy to a level above that of his brothers."

37:5–11. The spark of hatred kindled by Jacob's in-your-
face gift (37:4) bursts into a blaze when Joseph tells his dreams. Is
he brimming over with wonderment or boasting? Assuming the
worst, his brothers take the first dream as Joseph's arrogant
assertion of his ambition to "reign" over them (37:8; the verb
derives from the Hebrew word for *king*).

The second dream offends even Jacob, who thinks Joseph
is predicting that the entire family—Jacob, Rachel, the ten older
brothers, and the youngest, Benjamin—will bow down to him one
day (37:9–10). For a father in this patriarchal society to prostrate
himself before his son is a radically offensive idea. But Jacob's
interpretation is impossible: Joseph's mother, Rachel, is in her
grave (35:19). Perhaps there is more to Joseph's dreams than his
family has perceived.

37:12–28. Jacob's behavior is hard to explain. He sends
his precious son alone to Shechem, where the family has bitter
enemies (Genesis 34; see page 11). This also puts Joseph at the
mercy of his brothers, whose buildup of anger and breakdown in
communications (37:4) has somehow escaped Jacob.

If the sight of daddy's boy all decked out in his "I am
special" finery is hard for the brothers to take, it is the thought of
his dreams that triggers their urge to kill. They belittle Joseph as
"this dreamer" (the literal Hebrew—"this lord of dreams"—is

bitingly sarcastic: 37:19). The scorn masks a deep-seated fear. What if the dreams *are* prophetic? What if subservience to Joseph is in their future? To eliminate this nightmarish possibility, the brothers will eliminate the dreamer.

The plot takes on a life of its own. As one plan gives way to another, we see chinks in the brothers' outwardly united front and ponder some intriguing questions. What has made the brothers so savage that they will gleefully murder Joseph and deny him proper burial, the ultimate dishonor in their world (Plan One: 37:20)? Reuben pushes for sending Joseph to a lingering death in an empty "pit," or water cistern (Plan Two: 37:21–22), while secretly planning to save him. Why? Is Reuben trying to compensate for past sins (see 35:16–22)? Does he hope to gain Jacob's favor by aligning himself with Number One Son? Or has he realized that, as the eldest, he will be held accountable for any mishap?

Selling Joseph into slavery is Judah's bright idea (Plan Three: 37:26–28). What motivates him? money? second thoughts about bloodguilt? a sudden pang of concern for "our brother"? Literary critic Robert Alter wryly observes that "it is, of course, a dubious expression of brotherhood to sell someone into the ignominy and perilously uncertain future of slavery." (In later Jewish law, it was a capital offense: Exodus 21:16).

Verse 28 leaves us guessing about who actually makes a profit on Joseph. It may be the brothers, who interrupt their lunch to make a deal with the Ishmaelite caravan (37:25). Or is it Midianite traders who find and sell him?

37:29–36. In the end, the family is more unhappy than ever. Reuben, who seems to have been absent when Plan Three was hatched, is distraught (37:29–30). Jacob is inconsolable. His sons have deceived him easily, using their brother's garment and a goat—"evidence" reminiscent of the props with which Jacob once tricked his own father, Isaac (27:5–23). They will not find it easy to live with the ghost of Joseph's memory, which lives on in Jacob's unceasing laments (37:34–35).

As for Joseph, we know nothing of his thoughts as he travels toward Egypt. He is as inscrutable as the sphinx.

Questions for Application

40 minutes
Choose questions according to your interest and time.

1 Is it possible to love a person too much?

2 Scholar Laurence Turner observes that Joseph seems to possess one gift of wisdom—dreams—while lacking another—prudence. Do you agree?

3 How does envy affect a person's ability to make judgments and decisions? What are the warning signals that envy is eating at a relationship?

4 If you wanted to encourage someone's cherished hopes, desires, and ambitions, how would you go about it? What are some surefire ways of squelching another person's dreams?

5 When is solidarity—standing together with others—a force for good? What could you do to build solidarity within your home, parish, school, workplace, or community? When is solidarity not appropriate?

6 From your experience of giving and receiving comfort in times of sorrow, what kind of consolation is truly helpful? Do you know anyone who could use such consolation now? What might you do to comfort them?

7 For personal reflection: Is there anyone in your life to whom you just cannot "speak peaceably" (37:4)? Have you asked the Prince of Peace to bring healing to this relationship? How can you cooperate with his work?

You do not have to be an expert on Scripture to lead a group.

Clarence and Edith Roberts, *Sharing of Scripture*

Approach to Prayer

15 minutes
Use this approach—or create your own!

◆ With your closest relationships
in mind, read aloud these words
from 1 Corinthians 13:4–8, 13:

Love is patient; love is kind;
love is not envious or boastful
or arrogant or rude. It does not
insist on its own way; it is not
irritable or resentful; it does
not rejoice in wrongdoing, but
rejoices in the truth. It bears
all things, believes all things,
hopes all things, endures all
things. Love never ends. . . .
And now faith, hope, and love
abide, these three; and the
greatest of these is love.

Take a few silent moments to
present all your relationships to
the Lord and ask him to show
you what love means in each of
them. End with an Our Father.

Saints in the Making

The Power of a Dream

This section is a supplement for individual reading.

Does God still speak through dreams? Consider Alessandro Serenelli, whose daydreams led him into darkness—until another kind of dream showed him the light.

In 1902, Alessandro and his father were struggling tenant farmers living twenty miles from Rome. They shared a house with a widow and her six children. When not in the fields, twenty-year-old Alessandro was in his room reading sensationalized newspaper accounts of crimes of passion. As his mind filled with violent images, his lustful desires settled on eleven-year-old Maria. He made sexual overtures, which Maria rejected with a horrified no. He made threats: "If you tell your mother, I'll kill you."

One Saturday when Maria was alone in the house, Alessandro insisted that she have sex with him, or else. But even when he pulled out a dagger, Maria stood her ground: "No! No! What are you doing? Don't touch me! It's a sin! You'll go to hell!" Enraged, Alessandro stabbed her repeatedly, then threw himself sullenly on his bed. "I killed her because she refused," he later admitted. Maria was treated for fourteen major stab wounds and died the next day, after declaring that she forgave Alessandro.

Alessandro showed no remorse. A thirty-year prison sentence left him unmoved. Then one night, eight years later, Alessandro had a dream. He saw Maria, bathed in light, standing in a field of flowers. She was smiling and holding out an armful of radiantly white lilies. "Take them," she said. Alessandro's hardness of heart evaporated; he recognized the dream as God's invitation to repent. When the local bishop sought him out a few days later, Alessandro admitted his guilt and received God's forgiveness.

While in prison, Alessandro returned to the sacraments and to prayer. Released after serving twenty-seven years, he visited Maria's mother to beg her forgiveness, then spent the rest of his days working at a monastery and living a penitential life. "I hope to be able to save my soul, because I have a saint in heaven who is praying for me," Alessandro once told a priest. On June 24, 1950—almost three decades after the "mysterious, surprising dream" that precipitated his conversion—Alessandro saw his intuition confirmed. Along with Maria's family, he was present in St. Peter's Square in Rome as Maria Goretti was officially declared a saint.

Between Discussions

Not for Sunday School

O nce when Louise's mother was in her twenties, she asked the parish priest for advice about reading the Old Testament. "Don't," he told her. "There are things in it that you won't understand and that will only upset you." My guess is that he was referring to stories like the one in Genesis 38—the tale of Tamar and Judah. Certainly this story is not immediately edifying to the modern reader.

Postponing the story of Joseph in Egypt until chapter 39, the narrator follows the fortunes of Jacob's fourth son as he goes away from his brothers, finds himself a Canaanite wife, and quickly fathers three sons. Fast-forward twenty years or so. Judah's oldest son, Er, marries a local woman named Tamar. Before they have any children, and for unexplained reasons, Er incurs God's displeasure and dies (38:7). Some ancient rabbis speculated that Er did not want Tamar's beauty marred by pregnancy. Whatever motivated him, "Er erred," as one modern commentator remarks.

Judah then instructs his second son, Onan, to "perform the duty of a brother-in-law" to Tamar, that is, to have sexual relations with her in hopes of providing a son who can be counted as Er's firstborn (38:8). Odd-sounding to us, this legal obligation was widespread practice in the ancient Near East, where a family's quality of life and very survival hinged on the existence of an heir. Later Jewish law explained it as a measure to ensure that the deceased brother's name "may not be blotted out of Israel" (Deuteronomy 25:5–6).

Our English word *onanism* describes Son Number Two's response: on every occasion of intercourse with Tamar (the Hebrew makes it clear that this was not a onetime thing), he ejaculates on the ground "so that he would not give offspring to his brother" (38:8–9). No surprise that Onan, too, displeases God, and dies (38:10).

In contrast to Jacob's wild grieving over Joseph, Judah is not pictured as mourning his sons' deaths. Callous he may be, but certainly he fears for his third and last son, Shelah, who should step in to fulfill the obligation Onan refused (38:11). Perhaps holding Tamar responsible for his sons' deaths, Judah puts her off by telling her to wait until Shelah is older. But he has no intention of following through.

Judah's wife dies. Shelah grows up. Finally tiring of the charade, Tamar decides to provide Er with an heir by means of a highly risky and risqué plan. She disguises herself, tricks Judah into taking her for a prostitute, and has sex with him. First, however, she sets her price—one goat—and exacts Judah's seal, cord, and staff as a pledge of payment (38:18). She drives a hard bargain, Robert Alter observes. "Taking the instruments of Judah's legal identity and social standing is something like taking a person's driver's license and credit cards in modern society."

Tamar hangs on to these items, and good thing, too! On the day she is found to be pregnant and is denounced as an adulteress, Judah, without any reflection or call for evidence, sentences her to death, the usual penalty for adultery (Deuteronomy 22:22)—but by the unusually severe means of fire. In the story's dramatic climax, Tamar is being dragged off to the stake when she sends Judah's signet, cord, and staff back to him with the message: "It was the owner of these who made me pregnant. . . . Take note, please, whose these are" (38:25).

Judah gets the point and vindicates Tamar immediately: "She is more in the right than I, since I did not give her to my son Shelah" (38:26). If Tamar behaved unconventionally, Judah realizes, he himself was unjust. "Tamar opens Judah's eyes and teaches him to take responsibility and secure his family's future," comments scholar Ron Pirson. These will be valuable lessons for the future.

The story closes with the birth of Tamar's twins, Perez and Zerah—two boys who replace, as it were, Judah's lost sons. In time, Perez will head the clan of Judah from which King David will come. Thanks to Tamar's determination, Judah will have the honor of "fathering" not only David, but—through the legal fatherhood of Joseph of Nazareth—the Savior of the world (Matthew 1:2–16).

Keep your eye on Judah as the story of Joseph unfolds. The loss of his sons, his deception by Tamar, the chastening discovery that he is in the wrong and has almost condemned a courageous woman to death—all of this makes him a character to watch.

NOT YOUR BOY TOY

Questions to Begin

15 minutes
Use a question or two to get warmed up for the reading.

1   When was the last time you were blamed for something you didn't do? When was the last time you blamed someone for something it turned out *they* didn't do?

2   How important are good looks?

3   What's the worst job you ever had?

Opening the Bible

5 minutes
Read the passage aloud. Let individuals take turns reading
paragraphs.

The Reading: Genesis 39

Things Are Looking Up

1 Now Joseph was taken down to Egypt, and Potiphar, an officer of Pharaoh, the captain of the guard, an Egyptian, bought him from the Ishmaelites who had brought him down there. 2 The LORD was with Joseph, and he became a successful man; he was in the house of his Egyptian master. 3 His master saw that the LORD was with him, and that the LORD caused all that he did to prosper in his hands. 4 So Joseph found favor in his sight and attended him; he made him overseer of his house and put him in charge of all that he had. 5 From the time that he made him overseer in his house and over all that he had, the LORD blessed the Egyptian's house for Joseph's sake; the blessing of the LORD was on all that he had, in house and field. 6 So he left all that he had in Joseph's charge; and, with him there, he had no concern for anything but the food that he ate.

Things Fall Apart

Now Joseph was handsome and good-looking. 7 And after a time his master's wife cast her eyes on Joseph and said, "Lie with me." 8 But he refused and said to his master's wife, "Look, with me here, my master has no concern about anything in the house, and he has put everything that he has in my hand. 9 He is not greater in this house than I am, nor has he kept back anything from me except yourself, because you are his wife. How then could I do this great wickedness, and sin against God?" 10 And although she spoke to Joseph day after day, he would not consent to lie beside her or to be with her. 11 One day, however, when he went into the house to do his work, and while no one else was in the house, 12 she caught hold of his garment, saying, "Lie with me!" But he left his garment in her hand, and fled and ran outside. 13 When she saw that he had left his garment in her hand and had fled outside, 14 she called out to the members of her household and said to them, "See, my husband has brought among us a Hebrew to insult us! He came in to me to lie with me, and I cried out with a loud voice; 15 and when he heard me raise my voice and cry out, he left his garment beside me, and fled outside." 16 Then she kept his garment by her until his master came home, 17 and she told him the same story, saying, "The Hebrew servant, whom you have brought among us, came in to me to insult me; [18] but as soon as I raised my voice and cried out, he left his garment beside me, and fled outside."

[19] When his master heard the words that his wife spoke to him, saying, "This is the way your servant treated me," he became enraged. [20] And Joseph's master took him and put him into the prison, the place where the king's prisoners were confined; he remained there in prison.

Things Are Looking Up Again

[21] But the LORD was with Joseph and showed him steadfast love; he gave him favor in the sight of the chief jailer. [22] The chief jailer committed to Joseph's care all the prisoners who were in the prison, and whatever was done there, he was the one who did it. [23] The chief jailer paid no heed to anything that was in Joseph's care, because the LORD was with him; and whatever he did, the LORD made it prosper.

Questions for Careful Reading

10 minutes
Choose questions according to your interest and time.

1 Locate all the references to God in this chapter. What are the signs that "the LORD was with Joseph" (39:2)? How has the Lord been with him all along?

2 Why doesn't God's blessing of Joseph preserve him from suffering?

3 Compare 39:21 with 39:2. What new dimension has come into Joseph's experience of God's blessing? How did it get there?

4 What means does Joseph use to resist the advances of his master's wife? What motivates him?

5 Potiphar's wife tells her version of the story twice—once to the household slaves (39:14–15) and once to her husband (39:17–18). How does she adapt her story to each audience?

6 Reading between the lines, what can be surmised about Mr. and Mrs. Potiphar's marriage?

A Guide to the Reading

If participants have not read this section already, read it aloud. Otherwise go on to "Questions for Application."

39:1–6. This week's reading opens and closes with assertions that the Lord is with Joseph to help, bless, and make him successful in whatever he does (39:2–6, 21–23). This is our first indication that divine providence is at work in this story. It is troubling, then, that these assurances of God's favor frame a second major downturn in Joseph's fortunes. Seeing him slip from slave to prisoner, one is reminded of St. Teresa of Ávila's tart complaint to the Lord: "If this is how you treat your friends, no wonder you have so few of them."

Joseph's period of captivity opens as auspiciously as a slave could hope for. Early rabbinic commentators detected a providential softening of his suffering right from the beginning, as modern scholar Nahum M. Sarna explains: since his buyers were traders of fragrant goods (37:25), "at least, he was not subject to the usual malodors that characterized nomadic caravans"!

Joseph is sold to Potiphar, a high-placed government official with a large estate and a high-end lifestyle. He is spared the rigors of field labor and given work in the house, perhaps at some administrative task that showcases his managerial skills. Everything Joseph touches turns to gold. No wonder he is moved up the career ladder so quickly! Eager to cash in on Joseph's blessing, Potiphar assigns him wider and wider spheres of responsibility, which come to encompass everything but Potiphar's most personal affairs (39:6).

39:7–12. Potiphar looks approvingly on Joseph (39:3–4). For different reasons, so does his wife (39:6–7). Her wandering eyes note Joseph's drop-dead good looks (39:6). Liking what she sees, the master's wife demands it in the blunt manner of powerful people who get their way.

Joseph does not simply reject adultery as a "sin against God" (39:9) in its own right, though he undoubtedly sees it that way. More than this, he stresses his responsibility to honor the trust his master has placed in him—a trust he would break if he committed the "great wickedness" (39:9) of climbing into Potiphar's marriage bed. Joseph's primary defense against this sexual temptation seems to be his awareness of Potiphar's trust and favor. In a thought-provoking comment on this episode, Claus Westermann observes that "propriety in sexual matters depends on the strength of non-sexual relationships."

Is Mrs. Potiphar gorgeous or ugly? While it is impossible to know how much it costs Joseph to withstand her physical charms, we can at least appreciate the courage required to resist "day after day" pressure (39:10), especially when it comes from someone who can make or break him.

39:13–18. Potiphar's wife is a well-versed liar whose example offers instructive pointers to those similarly inclined. (1) *Act fast.* No time to wallow in anger, humiliation, or frustration. To save her skin, she must accuse Joseph before he can accuse her. (2) *Recruit witnesses.* The household slaves come running at her scream, which she presents as proof of her innocence (39:14, 18). To gain their support, she flatteringly associates them with herself and appeals to their suspicion of foreigners: this "Hebrew" has insulted "us" Egyptians. (3) *Twist the evidence.* The abandoned garment should incriminate her, but a few sly words transform it into a convincing prop for her story. (4) *Keep it plausible.* Lies are harder to detect when they depart from reality as little as possible. Cunningly, Potiphar's wife changes only a few critical details and makes her accusation using ambiguous, loaded words. In the Hebrew, "insult" can mean erotic play; "he came in to me" can mean either entering a room or having intercourse (39:14, 17). (5) *Shift the blame.* Though herself guilty of sexual assault, she charges Joseph with it. There is even an ambiguous hint of accusation against her husband for bringing Joseph into the house in the first place! Obviously, this couple has issues.

39:19–23. Even in prison, Joseph's divine blessing marks him out. Spotting it, the chief jailer responds exactly as Potiphar did and puts all his affairs in Joseph's hands.

The new note in Joseph's second rise to influence is his experience of God's "steadfast love," a term that describes a quality of loyalty (39:21). By his upright behavior toward the Potiphars, Joseph has demonstrated his commitment to the Lord. Because he has been faithful, he can now experience God's blessing in a relationship of mutual faithfulness.

Questions for Application

40 minutes
Choose questions according to your interest and time.

1 What is success? What do you think makes someone a success in life?

2 What is the difference between cooperating with God's grace and striving to earn God's favor through our own actions? How does each approach affect our relationship with God?

3 Spiritual writers and biblical commentators over the centuries have pointed out that Potiphar's wife is the real slave in this story. How can people know when they are becoming slaves to particular habits, thought patterns, relationships, sins?

4 Joseph has a strong grasp on right and wrong. How can adults help young people develop a healthy, well-formed conscience? How should adults pursue the lifelong task of educating, examining, and following their own conscience?

5 From your own experience, what are some effective ways of dealing with unavoidable temptations?

6 Potiphar punished Joseph without bothering to hear him out. When have you rushed to judgment without listening to two sides of a dispute? Why is it sometimes hard to remember that there are at least two sides to the stories we hear? What is helpful for avoiding rash judgments?

7 St. Caesarius of Arles observed that Joseph was not alone in his hour of need: "The Lord visits his own even in prison." When have you experienced God's presence in a time of suffering?

Everyone can take an hour from time to time to enter a church, sit before an icon at home, or go out into the solitude of nature. There, in silence, we can meditate on a passage of Scripture to listen to the voice of Christ.

The Taizé Community, *Listening with the Heart*

Approach to Prayer

15 minutes
Use this approach—or create your own!

◆ As a group, take just a few
minutes to mention various
groups of people around the
world who have been falsely
accused, deprived of rights,
victimized. (Your list might
include child laborers,
persecuted minorities, political
prisoners . . .) Bring these
people before God in prayer by
having someone read these
words from Psalm 10.

Why, O LORD, do you stand far
    off?
    Why do you hide yourself
      in times of
      trouble? . . .
Rise up, O LORD; O God, lift up
    your hand;
    do not forget the
      oppressed. . . .
O LORD, you will hear the desire
    of the meek;
    you will strengthen their
      heart, you will incline
      your ear
to do justice for the orphan and
    the oppressed.

End with an Our Father.

A Living Tradition

On Resisting Temptation

This section is a supplement for individual reading.

John Chrysostom, the fourth-century bishop of Constantinople (modern Istanbul), preached an instructive and entertaining series of homilies on Genesis. His discussion of Joseph and Potiphar's wife suggests practical responses to temptation.

◆ Concern for the other person. "Joseph was greatly concerned to deliver her from this folly and improper desire, as far as was possible. . . . He offered her advice calculated to awaken her to a sense of shame and make her realize what was for her good."

◆ Fear of the Lord. Joseph told Potiphar's wife: "Even if we succeed in escaping the notice of everyone, we will not be able to escape the notice of the unsleeping eye."

◆ Perseverance. "Not once or twice but many times he endured this pressure and resisted the invitation."

◆ Flight—when all else fails, it's honorable to run! While it was "remarkable that the three young men survived unharmed in the midst of the Babylonian furnace and sustained no harm from the fire [Daniel 3], it was remarkable and unprecedented that this young man had his clothes torn from him by this frenzied and intemperate woman without yielding to her and, leaving the clothes in her hands, fled the scene in that condition. You see, just as those three young men on account of their virtue received grace from on high . . . so this man, too, after making whatever effort he could and giving evidence of his struggle for continence with great intensity, enjoyed abundant help from on high and all at once prevailed. . . . Then one could see this remarkable man emerging, divested of his clothes but garbed in the vesture of chastity, as though escaping unharmed from some fiery furnace, not only not scorched by the flames but even more conspicuous and resplendent."

Chrysostom's practical suggestion for how to imitate Joseph: "Let us recall in every circumstance those words of Joseph, 'How could I do this wicked deed and commit sin in God's eyes?' So when some temptation disturbs us, let us turn these words over in our mind, and every unholy desire will immediately be put to flight."

TELL ME YOUR DREAMS

Questions to Begin

15 minutes
Use a question or two to get warmed up for the reading.

1 What's your favorite bakery item?

2 Do you think God still guides people through dreams? Has this happened to anyone you know?

Opening the Bible

5 minutes
Read the passage aloud. Let individuals take turns reading paragraphs.

The Reading: Genesis 40–41

Dreaming in Detention

40:1 Some time after this, the cupbearer of the king of Egypt and his baker offended their lord the king of Egypt. 2 Pharaoh was angry with his two officers, the chief cupbearer and the chief baker, 3 and he put them in custody in the house of the captain of the guard, in the prison where Joseph was confined. 4 The captain of the guard charged Joseph with them, and he waited on them. . . .

5 One night they both dreamed—the cupbearer and the baker of the king of Egypt, who were confined in the prison—each his own dream, and each dream with its own meaning. 6 When Joseph came to them in the morning, he saw that they were troubled. 7 So he asked Pharaoh's officers, who were with him in custody in his master's house, "Why are your faces downcast today?" 8 They said to him, "We have had dreams, and there is no one to interpret them." And Joseph said to them, "Do not interpretations belong to God? Please tell them to me."

9 So the chief cupbearer told his dream to Joseph, and said to him, "In my dream there was a vine before me, 10 and on the vine there were three branches. As soon as it budded, its blossoms came out and the clusters ripened into grapes. 11 Pharaoh's cup was in my hand; and I took the grapes and pressed them into Pharaoh's cup, and placed the cup in Pharaoh's hand."

12 Then Joseph said to him, "This is its interpretation: the three branches are three days; 13 within three days Pharaoh will lift up your head and restore you to your office; and you shall place Pharaoh's cup in his hand, just as you used to do when you were his cupbearer. 14 But remember me when it is well with you; please do me the kindness to make mention of me to Pharaoh, and so get me out of this place. 15 For in fact I was stolen out of the land of the Hebrews; and here also I have done nothing that they should have put me into the dungeon."

16 When the chief baker saw that the interpretation was favorable, he said to Joseph, "I also had a dream: there were three cake baskets on my head, 17 and in the uppermost basket there were all sorts of baked food for Pharaoh, but the birds were eating it out of

the basket on my head." 18 And Joseph answered, "This is its interpretation: the three baskets are three days; 19 within three days Pharaoh will lift up your head—from you! —and hang you on a pole; and the birds will eat the flesh from you."

20 On the third day, which was Pharaoh's birthday, he made a feast for all his servants, and lifted up the head of the chief cupbearer and the head of the chief baker among his servants. 21 He restored the chief cupbearer to his cupbearing, and he placed the cup in Pharaoh's hand; 22 but the chief baker he hanged, just as Joseph had interpreted to them. 23 Yet the chief cupbearer did not remember Joseph, but forgot him.

Pharaoh Is Frightened

41:1 After two whole years, Pharaoh dreamed that he was standing by the Nile, 2 and there came up out of the Nile seven sleek and fat cows, and they grazed in the reed grass. 3 Then seven other cows, ugly and thin, came up out of the Nile after them, and stood by the other cows on the bank of the Nile. 4 The ugly and thin cows ate up the seven sleek and fat cows. And Pharaoh awoke. 5 Then he fell asleep and dreamed a second time; seven ears of grain, plump and good, were growing on one stalk. 6 Then seven ears, thin and blighted by the east wind, sprouted after them. 7 The thin ears swallowed up the seven plump and full ears. Pharaoh awoke, and it was a dream.

8 In the morning his spirit was troubled; so he sent and called for all the magicians of Egypt and all its wise men. Pharaoh told them his dreams, but there was no one who could interpret them to Pharaoh.

9 Then the chief cupbearer said to Pharaoh, "I remember my faults today. 10 Once Pharaoh was angry with his servants, and put me and the chief baker in custody in the house of the captain of the guard. 11 We dreamed on the same night, he and I, each having a dream with its own meaning. 12 A young Hebrew was there with us, a servant of the captain of the guard. When we told him, he interpreted our dreams to us, giving an interpretation to each according to his dream. 13 As he interpreted to us, so it turned out; I was restored to my office, and the baker was hanged."

14 Then Pharaoh sent for Joseph, and he was hurriedly brought out of the dungeon. When he had shaved himself and changed his

clothes, he came in before Pharaoh. 15 And Pharaoh said to Joseph, "I have had a dream, and there is no one who can interpret it. I have heard it said of you that when you hear a dream you can interpret it." 16 Joseph answered Pharaoh, "It is not I; God will give Pharaoh a favorable answer."

17 Then Pharaoh said to Joseph, "In my dream I was standing on the banks of the Nile; 18 and seven cows, fat and sleek, came up out of the Nile and fed in the reed grass. 19 Then seven other cows came up after them, poor, very ugly, and thin. Never had I seen such ugly ones in all the land of Egypt. 20 The thin and ugly cows ate up the first seven fat cows, 21 but when they had eaten them no one would have known that they had done so, for they were still as ugly as before. Then I awoke. 22 I fell asleep a second time and I saw in my dream seven ears of grain, full and good, growing on one stalk, 23 and seven ears, withered, thin, and blighted by the east wind, sprouting after them; 24 and the thin ears swallowed up the seven good ears. . . ."

What It Means and What to Do about It

25 Then Joseph said to Pharaoh, "Pharaoh's dreams are one and the same; God has revealed to Pharaoh what he is about to do. 26 The seven good cows are seven years, and the seven good ears are seven years; the dreams are one. 27 The seven lean and ugly cows that came up after them are seven years, as are the seven empty ears blighted by the east wind. They are seven years of famine. . . .

29 "There will come seven years of great plenty throughout all the land of Egypt. 30 After them there will arise seven years of famine, and all the plenty will be forgotten in the land of Egypt; the famine will consume the land. . . . 32 And the doubling of Pharaoh's dream means that the thing is fixed by God, and God will shortly bring it about.

33 "Now therefore let Pharaoh select a man who is discerning and wise, and set him over the land of Egypt. 34 Let Pharaoh proceed to appoint overseers over the land, and take one-fifth of the produce of the land of Egypt during the seven plenteous years. 35 Let them gather all the food of these good years that are coming, and lay up grain under the authority of Pharaoh for food in the cities, and let them keep it. 36 That food shall be a reserve for the land against the seven years of famine that are to befall the land of Egypt. . . ."

Joseph Is Promoted

37 The proposal pleased Pharaoh and all his servants. 38 Pharaoh said to his servants, "Can we find anyone else like this—one in whom is the spirit of God?" 39 So Pharaoh said to Joseph, "Since God has shown you all this, there is no one so discerning and wise as you. 40 You shall be over my house, and all my people shall order themselves as you command; only with regard to the throne will I be greater than you. . . ." 42 Removing his signet ring from his hand, Pharaoh put it on Joseph's hand; he arrayed him in garments of fine linen, and put a gold chain around his neck. 43 He had him ride in the chariot of his second-in-command; and they cried out in front of him, "Bow the knee!" Thus he set him over all the land of Egypt.
44 Moreover Pharaoh said to Joseph, "I am Pharaoh, and without your consent no one shall lift up hand or foot in all the land of Egypt." 45 Pharaoh gave Joseph the name Zaphenath-paneah; and he gave him Asenath daughter of Potiphera, priest of On, as his wife. . . .

46 Joseph was thirty years old when he entered the service of Pharaoh king of Egypt. And Joseph went out from the presence of Pharaoh, and went through all the land of Egypt. 47 During the seven plenteous years the earth produced abundantly. 48 He gathered up all the food of the seven years when there was plenty in the land of Egypt, and stored up food in the cities. . . .

50 Before the years of famine came, Joseph had two sons, whom Asenath daughter of Potiphera, priest of On, bore to him. 51 Joseph named the firstborn Manasseh, "For," he said, "God has made me forget all my hardship and all my father's house." 52 The second he named Ephraim, "For God has made me fruitful in the land of my misfortunes."

53 The seven years of plenty that prevailed in the land of Egypt came to an end; 54 and the seven years of famine began to come, just as Joseph had said. There was famine in every country, but throughout the land of Egypt there was bread.

Questions for Careful Reading

10 minutes
Choose questions according to your interest and time.

1 Is Joseph's view of the source of dream interpretations different from the view of the cupbearer, the baker, and Pharaoh?

2 Why do you think the cupbearer forgot Joseph? Why did he suddenly remember him?

3 Compare the narrator's description of Pharaoh's dream with Pharaoh's own account (41:1–7, 17–24). What do the differences reveal about Pharaoh's state of mind?

4 What points are brought out by mentioning Joseph's two changes of clothing in chapter 41?

5 Does anything in this reading tell us how Joseph feels?

A Guide to the Reading

If participants have not read this section already, read it aloud. Otherwise go on to "Questions for Application."

40:1–8. After eleven years of enslavement, Joseph is still where he began—in a "pit" ("dungeon" in 40:15 is a translation of the same Hebrew word translated "pit" in 37:24). To all appearances, his brothers have succeeded in burying the promise of his youthful dreams. We have only two peepholes into Joseph's feelings about this (40:14–15; 41:51–52) and no information about how he now views his own dreams. Does he look back in anger and frustration? Or does he sense that some divine purpose is being served and will emerge in time?

Pharaoh's cupbearer and his baker are not kitchen drudges but VIPs awaiting sentencing.

Without telling the story of this duo's fall from favor, the narrator reports their troubled looks on a given morning. To his credit, Joseph is not so self-concerned as not to notice and inquire (40:7). Is this the same young man who seemed oblivious to his brothers' distress over Jacob's favoritism? Compassion is not the only new shoot growing in Joseph. He can now interpret other people's dreams. His insistence that "interpretations belong to God," along with his confidence that he has access to such information (40:8; 41:16), suggests that suffering has made Joseph more sensitive to the Lord, as well as to others.

40:9–23. Homing in on the essentials, Joseph reads the dreams as a contrasting pair of three-day forecasts. The cup-bearer's portrays active, successful service; the baker's is a negative image of passivity, incompetence, and failure (40:9–11, 16–17). Using a rather macabre pun, Joseph tells each dreamer that Pharaoh will "lift up your head." The expression refers to a ceremonial act of pardon for the cupbearer but announces bad news to the baker: he will be beheaded and impaled (40:13, 19).

When the cupbearer forgets Joseph's plea to "get me out of this place" (40:14, 23), Joseph hits rock bottom. It will be two more years and two more dreams before the cupbearer's memory is jogged by guilt, fear, or ambition (41:9–13).

41:1–36. Joseph's fortunes reverse with breathtaking speed. Grabbing a shave and a change of clothes, he is hustled before Pharaoh, who is still pinching himself to make sure he has awakened from the two nightmares his advisors have been unable (or afraid?) to interpret. Pharaoh smells trouble.

Like the previous pair of dreams, these include vivid images that involve food and numbers. But Joseph's interpretation brings out differences. The dreams refer not to days but to years and concern the future of millions.

Joseph's grim picture of famine raises questions about the "favorable answer" he said God would provide (41:16, 26–32). But before we have time to wonder whether this is a cruel joke, Joseph moves from dream interpretation to advising. The practical measures that he suggests (41:33–36) will ensure that Pharaoh derives the intended benefit of the divine warnings.

Successful implementation of these emergency measures hinges on Pharaoh's appointing a "discerning and wise" manager (41:33)—exactly the credentials that stand out on Joseph's resumé. Is he angling for the job?

41:37–54. For his part, Pharaoh endorses the whole package (41:38–39). Though fourteen years must pass before the interpretation is proven right or wrong, he detects "the spirit of God" both in Joseph's prophetic gift and his administrative abilities. Obviously, Pharaoh, too, has received some spiritual gift of discernment.

Pharaoh declares Joseph second-in-command and confers on him various insignia and honors (41:40–43). Thanks to archaeological finds, this is an event we can visualize "as very few others in the Bible story," says Claus Westermann. Egyptian representations picture "the almost transparent linen garments. We can view the rings, the golden chains, and the war chariots in the museums." Joseph's new Egyptian name and high-society wife mark a fresh start in life. Does it come at the price of forgetting his father and brothers? The name he gives his firstborn son makes us wonder (41:51). There is also the fact that, during seven years of occupying high office, Joseph has not once attempted to communicate with his family in Canaan.

But with the whole world famished and Egypt the only source of grain, he won't have to.

Questions for Application

40 minutes
Choose questions according to your interest and time.

1 The first step in Joseph's rise to power is a simple act of sympathy toward two prisoners. When have you seen a simple act of kindness lead to some unexpected larger good?

2 Does a person's own suffering necessarily make them more sensitive to the suffering of others?

3 Joseph's dark years gave him an opportunity to develop and demonstrate gifts he might never have exercised. When have opportunities come to you through difficult times? How has this affected your relationship with God?

4 Joseph seems certain that he can interpret the dreams of others. What makes him so sure? When is self-confidence a good thing?

5 How do you experience the presence of the Spirit in your life? How can Christians become more open to the Spirit living in them?

6 Do spiritual gifts always look "spiritual"? What are your God-given gifts? How are you using them?

7 For personal reflection: Is there some favor you've been asked to do that you've been putting off or forgetting? some request for prayer that someone has made of you? some practical service? Ask the Holy Spirit to jog your memory; then take appropriate action.

The fruit of Holy Scripture is . . . the fullness of eternal happiness.

St. Bonaventure

Approach to Prayer

15 minutes
Use this approach—or create your own!

◆ Everyone has prayers that they've been waiting on God to answer. Use this time to offer these intentions to God with trust and surrender. Ask someone to read this thought from the medieval mystic Julian of Norwich:

Sometimes it seems that we have been praying a long time and still do not have what we ask. But we should not be sad. I am sure that what our Lord means is that either we should wait for a better time, or more grace, or a better gift.

Take a few moments of silence; then invite members to mention whatever intentions they wish. After each one, the group might pray, "Lord, we put our hope in you." End with a Hail Mary.

A Living Tradition

Go to Joseph

This section is a supplement for individual reading.

One of our favorite statues of Joseph stands on a pedestal with an inscription that reads, *Ite ad Joseph*—Latin for Pharaoh's instructions to the people of Egypt about where to find grain during the famine: "Go to Joseph" (41:55). When this order was issued, Joseph undoubtedly resembled one of the figures depicted on ancient Egyptian wall carvings. His face and head were shaved, Egyptian-style, and he wore the chain and "fine linen" garment of a high official (41:14, 42). But our favorite statue doesn't have an Egyptian look at all. No, our statue shows a man with shoulder-length hair and a beard. He is wearing a simple brown robe. In his arms he holds a child. He is, of course, not Joseph of Egypt, but Joseph of Nazareth.

The narrator of the Joseph story in Genesis couldn't have foreseen that "Go to Joseph" would become a sort of slogan pointing to a much later provider of help. But the author of the first Gospel wouldn't have been a bit surprised. In his account of Jesus' birth and early life, Matthew highlighted a parallel between the two Josephs. Both men had fathers named Jacob; both had instructive dreams, demonstrated sexual restraint, and traveled to Egypt (Matthew 1:16, 20, 25; 2:13–15, 19–22). Most obviously, they shared the same name. In fact, as Scripture scholar Joseph Fitzmyer, S.J., points out, the parents of the second Joseph deliberately called their son after the first Joseph, who was celebrated for saving his family and people from starvation. In the last centuries before Jesus' birth, many Jewish boys were named after this famous guardian. As Fitzmyer notes, it turned out to be "a fitting name for the man who would play the role of guardian in the life of Jesus of Nazareth in the Christian Gospels."

Many centuries passed before Christian writers picked up on Matthew's connection of the two Josephs. Church Fathers often noted that the Old Testament Joseph prefigured Jesus, but only two of them briefly mentioned the correspondence between Old Testament Joseph and Jesus' adoptive father. Not until well into the twelfth century, when St. Bernard of Clairvaux preached a series of sermons highlighting Joseph of Nazareth's role in salvation history, did this comparison receive the attention it deserves. Bernard explained it this way:

And remember too that great patriarch who was sold once into Egypt. Realize that the Joseph we are speaking of here not only shared that other great man's name, but also imitated his chastity, closely resembling him in innocence and grace. The first Joseph, sold by jealous brothers and led off to Egypt, prefigured the selling of Christ. The second Joseph, fleeing jealous Herod, carried Christ away into Egypt. The first, keeping faith with the master, refused to couple with the mistress. The second, recognizing that the lady, the mother of the Lord, was a virgin, watched over her in faithful continence. The first had the gift of interpreting the hidden secrets of dreams. The second not only knew of heavenly mysteries but even participated in them. The first Joseph stored up grain for himself and for all the people; the second was given charge of the bread come down from heaven [John 6:41] for his sake and for that of the whole world.

St. Bernard's masterful treatment ensured that this comparison would be taken up and developed by others. According to Joseph Chorpenning, O.S.F.S., it played a pivotal role in New Testament Joseph's "gradual emergence from relative obscurity for over a millennium to one of the most venerated saints of the Roman Catholic Church by the seventeenth and eighteenth centuries."

Influential voices spoke up to enlarge on Bernard's approach and encourage personal devotion to St. Joseph. One of these was St. Francis de Sales, who acknowledged Bernard's influence in a sermon he gave on March 19, 1612, the Feast of St. Joseph. In it, he compared himself to the runners who preceded Old Testament Joseph's chariot crying out, "Bow the knee!" (41:43). "In truth, I also wish to go before our Joseph as herald," Francis admitted.

As Father Chorpenning explains, St. Francis developed the likeness "by a point by point comparison of the privileges conferred by Pharaoh upon the Old Testament patriarch and by God upon the new Joseph." The first—that Pharaoh set Joseph over his "house," to be obeyed by all the people (41:40)—signals St. Joseph's role as God the Father's right-hand man, "entrusted with God's family and ruling the Son of God and the Mother of God." The next three similarities are the gifts Pharaoh puts on Joseph (41:42). As Francis saw it, the signet ring relates to Joseph of Nazareth because it "identifies the man privy to all state secrets so that he may conduct its affairs. . . . Thus, the angel reveals to Joseph the secret of secrets" (see Matthew 1:20). The fine linen garments and gold chain symbolize, respectively, St. Joseph's "chaste robe of virginity" and "charity burning in his breast." Finally, the fact that Pharaoh places Joseph in a chariot (41:43) led Francis to see the very body of Joseph of Nazareth as a "chariot" especially entrusted to hold and carry God's own Son.

St. Francis's appreciation of St. Joseph was almost certainly fired by St. Teresa of Ávila. The influential sixteenth-century Carmelite took St. Joseph as her spiritual father after she was healed of a mysterious debilitating illness. Then, filled with "desire to persuade all to be devoted to him," she wrote about Joseph in books that Francis would have read.

Without ever using the phrase, St. Teresa advocated an energetic "Go to Joseph" approach. She took the step (unusual at the time) of putting St. Joseph's pictures and statues everywhere, named twelve monasteries after him, and insisted that he was an intercessor for every kind of need. "With other saints," wrote Teresa, "it seems the Lord has given them grace to be of help in one need, whereas with this glorious saint I have experience that he helps in all our needs."

Numerous other examples from Catholic tradition concerning Joseph's intercessory role could be cited, but perhaps the pithiest is this one, from Pius XII's 1955 announcement establishing the Feast of St. Joseph the Worker on May 1: "If you wish to be close to Christ, we again today repeat, '*Ite ad Joseph*— Go to Joseph.'"

It's still good advice.

WELL, LOOK WHO'S HERE

Questions to Begin

15 minutes
Use a question or two to get warmed up for the reading.

1 When was the last time you unexpectedly ran into a relative or old friend?

2 When have you unexpectedly gotten a product or service free of charge?

5 minutes
Read the passage aloud. Let individuals take turns reading
paragraphs.

The Reading: Genesis 42

To Egypt and Back

[1] Jacob . . . said to his sons, "Why do you keep looking at one another? [2] I have heard . . . that there is grain in Egypt; go down and buy grain for us there, that we may live and not die." [3] So ten of Joseph's brothers went down to buy grain in Egypt. [4] But Jacob did not send Joseph's brother Benjamin with his brothers, for he feared that harm might come to him. . . .

[6] Now Joseph was governor over the land; it was he who sold to all the people of the land. And Joseph's brothers came and bowed themselves before him with their faces to the ground. [7] When Joseph saw his brothers, he recognized them, but he treated them like strangers and spoke harshly to them. "Where do you come from?" he said. They said, "From the land of Canaan, to buy food." [8] Although Joseph had recognized his brothers, they did not recognize him. [9] Joseph also remembered the dreams that he had dreamed about them.

He said to them, "You are spies; you have come to see the nakedness of the land!" [10] They said to him, "No, my lord; your servants have come to buy food. [11] We are all sons of one man; we are honest men; your servants have never been spies." [12] But he said to them, "No, you have come to see the nakedness of the land!" [13] They said, "We, your servants, are twelve brothers, the sons of a certain man in the land of Canaan; the youngest, however, is now with our father, and one is no more." [14] But Joseph said to them, "It is just as I have said to you; you are spies! [15] Here is how you shall be tested: as Pharaoh lives, you shall not leave this place unless your youngest brother comes here! [16] Let one of you go and bring your brother, while the rest of you remain in prison, in order that your words may be tested, whether there is truth in you; or else, as Pharaoh lives, surely you are spies." [17] And he put them all together in prison for three days.

[18] On the third day Joseph said to them, "Do this and you will live, for I fear God: [19] if you are honest men, let one of your brothers stay here where you are imprisoned. The rest of you shall go and carry grain for the famine of your households, [20] and bring your youngest brother to me. Thus your words will be verified, and you shall not die." And they agreed to do so.

21 They said to one another, "Alas, we are paying the penalty for what we did to our brother; we saw his anguish when he pleaded with us, but we would not listen. That is why this anguish has come upon us.". . . 23 They did not know that Joseph understood them, since he spoke with them through an interpreter. 24 He turned away from them and wept; then he returned and spoke to them. And he picked out Simeon and had him bound before their eyes. 25 Joseph then gave orders to fill their bags with grain, to return every man's money to his sack, and to give them provisions for their journey. This was done for them.

26 They loaded their donkeys with their grain, and departed. 27 When one of them opened his sack to give his donkey fodder at the lodging place, he saw his money at the top of the sack. 28 He said to his brothers, "My money has been put back; here it is in my sack!" At this they lost heart and turned trembling to one another, saying, "What is this that God has done to us?"

29 When they came to their father Jacob in the land of Canaan, they told him . . . 30 "The man, the lord of the land, spoke harshly to us, and charged us with spying on the land. 31 But we said to him, 'We are honest men, we are not spies. 32 We are twelve brothers, sons of our father; one is no more, and the youngest is now with our father in the land of Canaan.' 33 Then the man, the lord of the land, said to us, 'By this I shall know that you are honest men: leave one of your brothers with me, take grain for the famine of your households, and go your way. 34 Bring your youngest brother to me, and I shall know that you are not spies but honest men. Then I will release your brother to you, and you may trade in the land.'"

35 As they were emptying their sacks, there in each one's sack was his bag of money. When they and their father saw their bundles of money, they were dismayed. 36 And their father Jacob said to them, "I am the one you have bereaved of children: Joseph is no more, and Simeon is no more, and now you would take Benjamin. All this has happened to me! . . . 38 My son shall not go down with you, for his brother is dead, and he alone is left. If harm should come to him on the journey that you are to make, you would bring down my gray hairs with sorrow to Sheol."

Questions for Careful Reading

10 minutes
Choose questions according to your interest and time.

1 How long has it been since Joseph last saw his brothers? (See 37:2; 41:46–47, 53.)

2 Jacob keeps Benjamin home because he fears that "harm might come to him" (42:4). What does this imply about Jacob? about the trip to Egypt?

3 Is Joseph's accusation of spying (42:9–16) simply the first thing that pops into his head or part of a plan?

4 Does Joseph seem different from when the story began? If so, what has contributed to the change?

5 Carefully compare the narrative (42:6–28) with the brothers' account to their father (42:30–34). What details do the brothers soften or omit? Why do they make these adjustments?

6 Jacob favored Rachel's son Joseph. Is Jacob now showing a preference for Rachel's other son, Benjamin? Cite specific evidence.

A Guide to the Reading

If participants have not read this section already, read it aloud. Otherwise go on to "Questions for Application."

42:1–17. The brothers need paternal prodding to get on their way to Egypt. They seem slow to grasp the obvious solution to their food shortage. Joseph's mind, by contrast, operates at warp speed. When his brothers unexpectedly appear, he instantly sizes up the situation, decides to conceal himself from them, and begins to give them a hard time. One commentator remarks that Joseph's family has a way of bringing out the worst in him.

Joseph's charge of spying catches the brothers off guard and sends them into a rambling defense. "They assert their innocence as if it were self-evident that the charge could not apply to them," biblical scholar George W. Coats observes. They insist they are brothers because brothers would be unlikely to endanger their whole family by engaging in anything as dangerous as espionage. Telling Joseph "we are all sons of one man" (42:11), they speak more truth than they realize! Another scholar, W. Lee Humphreys, remarks that it is amusing to see these men who were believed when they lied (37:31–33) now treated as liars when they speak the truth (42:7–14). As the brothers bow before Joseph in a customary ancient Near Eastern gesture of respect, they seem to be fulfilling his dreams.

For three days Joseph puts his brothers in a pressure cooker of confusion, anxiety, and conflict (42:15–17). You can almost hear them talking in their dark jail cell. "If this Egyptian official thinks we are spies, why is he willing to let *any* of us go back to Canaan?" "Which of us will go?" "And how can we trust that one to return for the rest of us?" And most urgently, because one man with a donkey cannot carry enough food for all their dependents: "What will happen to our families?"

42:18–25. Joseph seems to have changed his mind. Perhaps he has considered the impossibility of the family in Canaan surviving without food or their menfolk. Perhaps, too, he has pictured the shock his elderly father would suffer at the sight of only one returning son.

Yet Joseph's revised plan is hardly kind. He can easily foresee that Jacob will refuse to allow Benjamin to be taken into the power of a hostile and unpredictable Egyptian official. This means that Simeon will stay in prison. Joseph knows that the famine will close on the family like a vise. One does not have to be a prophet to predict that when they face starvation, father and sons will argue over Benjamin. Egypt is the only source of food, and the brothers will insist on taking Benjamin there to save the family from starvation. In the meantime, watching the family's stores of food diminish, Jacob will dread the inevitable crisis.

Caught in a seemingly absurd trap, the brothers feel that God must be punishing them for their sins. Naturally their worst sin comes to mind (42:21–22). In their recollection of the attack on Joseph we hear for the first time of his pathetic appeals to them when they threw him in the pit (37:23–24).

Joseph weeps. Is he pained by the reopening of the old wound? touched by the brothers' admission of guilt—and by a desire to be reconciled with them? Or does he turn aside to flush out his tender feelings with tears so as to be able to continue to coolly exact revenge? Is he perhaps torn by conflicting emotions? As readers, we observe Joseph at close range, yet from the outside. We see his tear-streaked face—but what is going on inside him?

42:26–38. The returned silver raises more questions. Is this Joseph's way of tempering harshness with generosity? Or is he planting evidence of theft, to make the brothers doubly fearful when they are forced to return to Egypt?

The brothers cover the miles toward home with foreboding. Long ago, they brought their father evidence of the death of a son and watched with horror as it drove him into unconsolable sorrow. How will he respond to their news about Simeon—and Benjamin?

The final scene is shot through with fear. The brothers are disturbed by the uncanny appearance of their money in all their sacks. Jacob is so distraught by their report that he comes unwittingly to the brink of accusing them of having taken Joseph from him (42:36). The last word of this troubling episode expresses the tone of foreboding: "Sheol"—the shadowy realm of the dead.

Questions for Application

40 minutes
Choose questions according to your interest and time.

1   Is Joseph taking revenge on his brothers? Would that be wrong? What is the attraction in revenge?

2   How does a guilty conscience affect a person's perception of events and of other people?

3   When is it appropriate to protect family members from bad news? When is it inappropriate?

4   How are parents affected by conflicts among their adult children? Should siblings avoid conflicts with each other for their parents' sake?

5   Jacob views events in the family in terms of how they affect *him* (42:36–38). What effect does a person who looks at situations this way have on his or her family? How can a person move beyond this outlook?

6 The troubles between Joseph and his brothers occurred two decades before the incidents in this week's reading. What kinds of long-term impact may problems between family members have on them? In what ways can wise decisions and good actions in a family also have long-term effects?

7 Where is God in this reading?

8 For personal reflection: Choose one of these questions and consider how it touches your life. What is God calling you to do in this area? Pray about this.

In order to activate the biblical texts, the reader has to become active. This requires paying attention to yourself, to your own responses, as you pay attention to the texts, and entering into two-way communication with them.

H. A. Nielsen, *The Bible—As If for the First Time*

Approach to Prayer

15 minutes
Use this approach—or create your own!

◆ Pray for families in difficult situations. Begin with the following prayer.

Wise and loving God, you created family life to be a place of growth and joy, a source of strength and comfort, a community where you dwell among us. Give your help and grace to families in need of resources, healing, and hope.

Pause silently. Then take turns praying these petitions (feel free to add to the list), concluding each item as a group with "Lord, have mercy."

Gracious God, we pray for families torn apart by lies, unfaithfulness, or abuse . . .
For families grieving the loss of a loved one . . .
For families where there is hunger or sickness . . .
For families where someone needs to be willing to take responsibility for wrongdoing . . .
For families where someone needs to forgive . . .
For all of us, with our weaknesses and failings toward one another . . .

End with an Our Father.

Saints in the Making

Reading from Experience

This section is a supplement for individual reading.

In his commentary on Genesis, when German biblical scholar Claus Westermann came to Joseph's questioning of his brothers (42:12–14), he recognized something he knew from experience. "The description of the interrogation shows an extraordinary . . . awareness on the part of the narrator," he wrote. "In an interrogation of this kind, the accused is defenseless, and the interrogator can take advantage of this lack of defense and beat the accused down by persistent hammering. It is disturbing that nothing has changed down to the present day."

Westermann, a German who was opposed to the Nazi regime, was drafted into the German army during World War II. He was taken captive in Russia and spent time in a Soviet prisoner of war camp, where brutal interrogations were not unusual. German prisoners in the Soviet Union had little chance of survival. Sitting in the prison camp, Westermann later wrote, he pondered the psalms "in a totally unacademic way."

At several points in his Genesis commentary, Westermann's wartime experiences seem to have made him sensitive to details that other readers might pass by. It strikes Westermann as remarkable that Joseph noticed that the cupbearer and the baker were downcast (40:7). Joseph's question about their gloomy looks was an ordinary expression of human concern, Westermann writes. But "one can only gauge the significance of such a question when one knows what the atmosphere of a prison is," where it is not easy to see beyond one's own suffering.

Westermann finds significance in Joseph's choice of a single word. After giving the cupbearer a promising interpretation of his dream, Joseph asks for his help to get out of the "dungeon" (40:15). Westermann writes that this is a "passionate statement." Joseph does not describe the place of confinement as a "prison," as seen from the "official" point of view, but as a hole, a pit, as seen from the point of view of the prisoner.

Westermann's commentary illustrates how a person's experiences in life prepare him or her to identify with the people in the biblical stories and understand their situations. Since each reader lives a unique life, each brings a unique awareness to the biblical text. In discussion of the Bible, this is one good reason for listening carefully to each others' observations.

Between Discussions

What's Joseph Up To?

In our most recent reading, Joseph harasses and bewilders his brothers. From his position of control, he unleashes waves of unpredictable events upon them. Their innocent search for food is met with false accusations. Unexpectedly they are put in jail. Equally unexpectedly, most of them are soon released. Sent packing as accused spies, they nevertheless receive their food free of charge. A strange power seems to have taken hold of their lives. They are baffled and afraid (42:21, 28, 35). In our next reading, Joseph continues to yank his brothers around with acts of unexplained graciousness and harshness. Although as readers we know more about what is happening than the brothers do, we, too, must wonder what Joseph is trying to accomplish.

The usual explanation is that Joseph is aiming at reconciliation with his brothers. "At the very moment that he saw his brothers before him," writes Claus Westermann, "Joseph decided to heal the breach." We might call this the "Merciful Joseph" explanation.

It may be asked why, once Joseph hears his brothers acknowledge their guilt for having sold him into slavery (42:21–22), he could not be reconciled with them simply by revealing himself and offering them forgiveness for their crime against him. A common answer is that lasting reconciliation will be possible only if the brothers demonstrate true repentance. Therefore Joseph creates a test to determine whether they have changed. He maneuvers them into a situation where they are tempted to abandon their father's other favored son, Benjamin. If they overcome the temptation, it will be clear that they have repented of the envy that drove them to get rid of Joseph.

Through the centuries, most readers have found that mercy is the most satisfactory explanation of Joseph's behavior. This explanation fits well with the uprightness that Joseph displays in his confrontation with Potiphar's wife (chapter 39) and, ultimately, in his generous behavior toward his brothers at the resolution of the story (chapter 45).

Some aspects of the story, however, are hard to square with the picture of a Merciful Joseph. At least to some readers, there seems to be something ruthless about Joseph's treatment of his brothers. One commentator draws attention to "the span of time during which they are forced to stew in agony over a fate that looms so strangely over them, and the manner in which he plays upon their guilt." In the view of another commentator, Joseph "lords it over his cowering fearful brethren, and plays with them as a cat plays with a mouse." Those who view Joseph as merciful reply that his harshness is a necessary part of his plan for good. Since the brothers' wickedness is deep-seated, only strong measures can determine whether they have really turned away from it.

Yet Jacob's treatment of his brothers brings suffering not only to them but also to his father. Why would a merciful Joseph torment his father? (What if elderly Jacob were to collapse under the strain of anxiety over sending Benjamin to Egypt?) And other questions may be raised. Is jailing Simeon for an indefinite period of time motivated by a desire for reconciliation with him? (What if he were to become sick and die in the dungeon?) After playing a wily game with his brothers, could Joseph expect his brothers ever to trust him again? One commentator remarks that "Joseph subjects his family to such severe treatment that any reconciliation is threatened." Besides, even if Joseph's treatment of his brothers is motivated by a desire for reconciliation, he hardly sets an example for how to go about healing broken family relationships.

The objections to the Merciful Joseph explanation lead some readers to the view that Joseph is bent on revenge. Robert Alter asks, "Does Joseph now feel anger and an impulse to punish his brothers, or is he chiefly triumphant, moved to play the inquisitor in order to act out still further the terms of his dreams, in which the brothers must repeatedly address him self-effacingly as 'my lord' and identify themselves as 'your servants'?" To these questions, some readers would answer yes and yes. Joseph is unfolding a dark plan, intending ultimately to enslave his brothers—or worse.

But objections may be raised against this Harsh Joseph interpretation also. If Joseph is seeking revenge, why the elaborate plan? Why not simply terrify his brothers by revealing himself and punish them at once? Perhaps, goes one answer, he is concerned for Benjamin's safety, so he manipulates the ten brothers into bringing Benjamin to Egypt, where Benjamin will be safe with him, after which he will take his revenge on the ten.

The most weighty objection to the Harsh Joseph explanation is that Joseph is portrayed elsewhere in the story as a man of integrity who is blessed and guided by God. Scheming to exact personal vengeance hardly fits this portrait.

A third possibility may be suggested: Joseph is both merciful and vengeful. Part of him would like to heal the breach with his brothers, but another part of him would like to make them suffer the way they made him suffer. This Conflicted Joseph is inclined both to help his brothers and to hurt them. He wavers back and forth between thoughts of reconciliation and thoughts of revenge.

Evidence for this interpretation is Joseph's apparent lack of resolution when his brothers arrive in Egypt. At first he puts the brothers in prison, with the directive that one of them should go home and fetch Benjamin—a decision that spells disaster for their starving families. Even though he swears by Pharaoh to carry through on this course of action (42:15), he soon reverses himself. Three days later, he releases all the brothers except Simeon, enabling them to bring enough food for their starving families (42:18–20). In the three days between these decisions, did Joseph move from a plan of vengeance to one of testing? Possibly. And after this point, did he continue to swing back and forth between punishing his brothers and moving toward reconciliation? That, too, seems possible.

Certainly, some of Joseph's actions in our last reading are open to more than one interpretation. His tears (42:24) may signal his rejection of vengeance. Or they may be an emotional release that enables him to pursue his cruel plan with calm self-control. Or they may express emotional chaos—hurt, anger, sadness, compassion, longing for reconciliation all fighting in his heart. Joseph's putting the brothers' money back in their sacks may be an act of kindness or a way of keeping them off balance by making them feel that the world has suddenly become weird—or the replaced money may be *both* a token of care and an instrument of disorientation. Perhaps Joseph's dealings with his brothers seem ambiguous to us because he himself is undecided about how his game with his brothers should turn out.

Biblical scholar Ron Pirson suggests that the appearance of his brothers after so many years sets off an inner struggle in Joseph. "Joseph has indeed retained genuine love for his family, but during his Egyptian years he has suppressed his feelings for his family—as has become manifest in the naming of his firstborn [41:51]. He is subject to an internal conflict: he is torn between the love for his family and the life he has led so far at the royal court without his father and his brothers. Now he has a family of his own: a wife, two sons, and Pharaoh (to whom he has become a father, 45:8). From the moment his brothers appear before his eyes, his emotions begin to become unwound (as seen by his weeping)—his spirit, however, does not want to give in. Little by little the family ties get the better of him."

It is hard to prove that any one interpretation is right and the others are wrong. The narrator brings us close to Joseph, closer than the brothers get. We hear him giving his steward secret instructions; we see him weeping in private. But the narrator does not bring us inside his mind and heart. Joseph remains something of an enigma. Not even the ending of the story will provide a conclusive answer to the question of his intentions, for we cannot be certain that things turn out as he planned. It may be that his plans are overturned by an unexpected event (our next reading may contain one), in which case, we can never be sure what his intended outcome would have been.

As we seek to understand the enigma of Joseph, we may also examine the enigma of ourselves. In what relationships do we waver between forgiveness and a desire for revenge? Why do we waver?

TAKE ME INSTEAD

Questions to Begin

15 minutes
Use a question or two to get warmed up for the reading.

---

1   When you were growing up, what was the seating arrangement at family meals?

---

2   When you were growing up, were there times when the whole class at school or all the children in the family had to suffer a punishment for something that only one person had done? (Were you ever that person?)

---

3   Describe a situation in which you successfully persuaded one of your parents to do something. How did it turn out?

Opening the Bible

5 minutes
Read the passage aloud. Let individuals take turns reading
paragraphs.

The Reading: Genesis 43–44

A Hard Choice

43:1 Now the famine was severe in the land. 2 And when they had eaten up the grain that they had brought from Egypt, their father said to them, "Go again, buy us a little more food." 3 But Judah said to him, "The man solemnly warned us, saying, 'You shall not see my face unless your brother is with you.' 4 If you will send our brother with us, we will go down and buy you food; 5 but if you will not send him, we will not go down. . . ." 6 Israel said, "Why did you treat me so badly as to tell the man that you had another brother?" 7 They replied, "The man questioned us carefully about ourselves and our kindred, saying, 'Is your father still alive? Have you another brother?' What we told him was in answer to these questions. Could we in any way know that he would say, 'Bring your brother down'?" 8 Then Judah said to his father Israel, "Send the boy with me, and let us be on our way, so that we may live and not die—you and we and also our little ones. 9 I myself will be surety for him; you can hold me accountable for him. If I do not bring him back to you and set him before you, then let me bear the blame forever. 10 If we had not delayed, we would now have returned twice."

11 Then their father Israel said to them, "If it must be so, then do this: take some of the choice fruits of the land in your bags, and carry them down as a present to the man—a little balm and a little honey, gum, resin, pistachio nuts, and almonds. 12 Take double the money with you. Carry back with you the money that was returned in the top of your sacks; perhaps it was an oversight. 13 Take your brother also, and be on your way again to the man; 14 may God Almighty grant you mercy before the man, so that he may send back your other brother and Benjamin. As for me, if I am bereaved of my children, I am bereaved." 15 So the men took the present, and they took double the money with them, as well as Benjamin. Then they went on their way down to Egypt, and stood before Joseph.

16 When Joseph saw Benjamin with them, he said to the steward of his house, "Bring the men into the house, and slaughter an animal and make ready, for the men are to dine with me at noon." 17 The man did as Joseph said, and brought the men to Joseph's house.

¹⁸ Now the men were afraid because they were brought to Joseph's house, and they said, "It is because of the money, replaced in our sacks the first time, that we have been brought in, so that he may have an opportunity to fall upon us, to make slaves of us and take our donkeys." ¹⁹ So they went up to the steward of Joseph's house and spoke with him at the entrance to the house. ²⁰ They said, "Oh, my lord, we came down the first time to buy food; ²¹ and when we came to the lodging place we opened our sacks, and there was each one's money in the top of his sack, our money in full weight. So we have brought it back with us. ²² Moreover we have brought down with us additional money to buy food. We do not know who put our money in our sacks."

²³ He replied, "Rest assured, do not be afraid; your God and the God of your father must have put treasure in your sacks for you; I received your money." Then he brought Simeon out to them. ²⁴ When the steward had brought the men into Joseph's house, and given them water, and they had washed their feet, and when he had given their donkeys fodder, ²⁵ they made the present ready for Joseph's coming at noon, for they had heard that they would dine there.

An Amazing Dinner

²⁶ When Joseph came home, they brought him the present that they had carried into the house, and bowed to the ground before him. ²⁷ He inquired about their welfare, and said, "Is your father well, the old man of whom you spoke? Is he still alive?" ²⁸ They said, "Your servant our father is well; he is still alive." And they bowed their heads and did obeisance. ²⁹ Then he looked up and saw his brother Benjamin, his mother's son, and said, "Is this your youngest brother, of whom you spoke to me? God be gracious to you, my son!" ³⁰ With that, Joseph hurried out, because he was overcome with affection for his brother, and he was about to weep. So he went into a private room and wept there. ³¹ Then he washed his face and came out; and controlling himself he said, "Serve the meal."

³² They served him by himself, and them by themselves, and the Egyptians who ate with him by themselves, because the Egyptians could not eat with the Hebrews, for that is an abomination to the Egyptians. ³³ When they were seated before him, the firstborn according to his birthright and the youngest according to his youth,

the men looked at one another in amazement. ³⁴ Portions were taken to them from Joseph's table, but Benjamin's portion was five times as much as any of theirs. So they drank and were merry with him.

Another False Accusation

^{44:1} Then he commanded the steward of his house, "Fill the men's sacks with food, as much as they can carry, and put each man's money in the top of his sack. ² Put my cup, the silver cup, in the top of the sack of the youngest, with his money for the grain." And he did as Joseph told him. ³ As soon as the morning was light, the men were sent away with their donkeys. ⁴ When they had gone only a short distance from the city, Joseph said to his steward, "Go, follow after the men; and when you overtake them, say to them, 'Why have you returned evil for good? Why have you stolen my silver cup? ⁵ Is it not from this that my lord drinks? Does he not indeed use it for divination? You have done wrong in doing this.'"

⁶ When he overtook them, he repeated these words to them. ⁷ They said to him, "Why does my lord speak such words as these? Far be it from your servants that they should do such a thing! ⁸ Look, the money that we found at the top of our sacks, we brought back to you from the land of Canaan; why then would we steal silver or gold from your lord's house? ⁹ Should it be found with any one of your servants, let him die; moreover the rest of us will become my lord's slaves." ¹⁰ He said, "Even so; in accordance with your words, let it be: he with whom it is found shall become my slave, but the rest of you shall go free." ¹¹ Then each one quickly lowered his sack to the ground, and each opened his sack. ¹² He searched, beginning with the eldest and ending with the youngest; and the cup was found in Benjamin's sack. ¹³ At this they tore their clothes. Then each one loaded his donkey, and they returned to the city.

¹⁴ Judah and his brothers came to Joseph's house while he was still there; and they fell to the ground before him. ¹⁵ Joseph said to them, "What deed is this that you have done? Do you not know that one such as I can practice divination?" ¹⁶ And Judah said, "What can we say to my lord? What can we speak? How can we clear ourselves? God has found out the guilt of your servants; here we are then, my lord's slaves, both we and also the one in whose possession the cup has been found." ¹⁷ But he said, "Far be it from me that I should do

so! Only the one in whose possession the cup was found shall be my slave; but as for you, go up in peace to your father."

A Cry from the Heart

18 Then Judah stepped up to him and said, "O my lord, let your servant please speak a word in my lord's ears, and do not be angry with your servant; for you are like Pharaoh himself. 19 My lord asked his servants, saying, 'Have you a father or a brother?' 20 And we said to my lord, 'We have a father, an old man, and a young brother, the child of his old age. His brother is dead; he alone is left of his mother's children, and his father loves him.' 21 Then you said to your servants, 'Bring him down to me, so that I may set my eyes on him.' 22 We said to my lord, 'The boy cannot leave his father, for if he should leave his father, his father would die.' 23 Then you said to your servants, 'Unless your youngest brother comes down with you, you shall see my face no more.'

24 "When we went back to your servant my father we told him the words of my lord. 25 And when our father said, 'Go again, buy us a little food,' 26 we said, 'We cannot go down. Only if our youngest brother goes with us, will we go down; for we cannot see the man's face unless our youngest brother is with us.' 27 Then your servant my father said to us, 'You know that my wife bore me two sons; 28 one left me, and I said, Surely he has been torn to pieces; and I have never seen him since. 29 If you take this one also from me, and harm comes to him, you will bring down my gray hairs in sorrow to Sheol.' 30 Now therefore, when I come to your servant my father and the boy is not with us, then, as his life is bound up in the boy's life, 31 when he sees that the boy is not with us, he will die; and your servants will bring down the gray hairs of your servant our father with sorrow to Sheol. 32 For your servant became surety for the boy to my father, saying, 'If I do not bring him back to you, then I will bear the blame in the sight of my father all my life.'

33 "Now therefore, please let your servant remain as a slave to my lord in place of the boy; and let the boy go back with his brothers. 34 For how can I go back to my father if the boy is not with me? I fear to see the suffering that would come upon my father."

Questions for Careful Reading

10 minutes
Choose questions according to your interest and time.

1 How would you explain the sequence of Joseph's questions in 43:27?

2 Is it possible for the brothers to do what Joseph tells them to do in 44:17?

3 In 44:18–34, does Judah speak just for himself or as spokesman for all the brothers? (Cite specific evidence.)

4 Does Judah's statement in 44:27–28 contain information Joseph could have known already? What effect might it have on Joseph?

5 For whose sake is Judah willing to take Benjamin's place in slavery?

6 Has Judah changed since the beginning of the story? If so, what has contributed to the change?

7 What does God do in this reading?

A Guide to the Reading

If participants have not read this section already, read it aloud.
Otherwise go on to "Questions for Application."

43:1–15. The family has run out of food. If we can take Judah's words literally, father and sons have been arguing for a month over what to do (43:10: two two-week round-trips between Canaan and Egypt). Jacob's attention is fixed solely on getting something to eat (43:2); he expresses no concern for Simeon—a contrast with his concern for Benjamin that the brothers cannot fail to notice.

Judah steps forward to shoulder responsibility for the situation. The last we heard of him he was straightening out a problem with his daughter-in-law Tamar (chapter 38), an episode in which he did not cut a heroic figure but did emerge with some integrity. From Tamar he learned that it is sometimes necessary to take risks in order to keep the family going. Now he urges this lesson on his father. Jacob must risk losing Benjamin, or else the whole family will certainly perish. Judah is willing to accept the emotional and spiritual burden of guilt if Benjamin is lost (43:9)— the kind of burden, we know, that he already bears for the loss of Joseph. By taking responsibility for Benjamin, Judah begins in some measure to reverse his crime against Joseph.

Born before the beginning of the story of Joseph (35:16–20), Benjamin must be at least in his twenties by this time. Yet his brothers continue to call him a "boy" (43:8). We are reminded of an elderly relative who, when he was a child, was called Sonny by his siblings. They continued to call him Sonny for the rest of their long lives.

Jacob loads his sons with local items of trade. The length of the gift list is a measure of his anxiety over what the powerful Egyptian official might do to his sons. All these items were on the manifest of the Ishmaelite caravan (37:25; 43:11), with the addition of a few pastry ingredients (almonds, pistachios, honey— did the Egyptians have a sweet tooth?) That long-ago caravan took one brother into slavery in Egypt. As we watch this new caravan set out to rescue a brother from Egypt, we may wonder whether it will also repair the terrible rupture in the family that occurred on the earlier occasion.

43:16–25. If we were expecting a speedy resolution, our hopes are dashed by Joseph's indifferent reaction to the brothers' arrival. He seems too busy to stop for a greeting. "There follows an assortment of digressions and frustrations that tease our curiosity," Meir Sternberg observes. "The plot creeps forward (43:18–44:3) to apparently little effect except to worsen our anxiety." Among the minor matters that suddenly loom large at this crucial moment are the donkeys (43:18, 24)! They not only slow down the plot but also remind us of the social gulf that now separates the ten brothers, who work with animals, from their high-class brother, who sits at the pinnacle of Egyptian society.

The unexpectedly warm reception by Joseph's steward stirs the brothers' suspicions. But when they defensively bring up the subject of the returned money, he dismisses their concern with a nonexplanation (imagine a bank teller telling you that angels put one thousand dollars in your checking account). Yet, as scholar Gerhard von Rad points out, the steward puts his finger on the "innermost mystery of the whole Joseph story: God's concealed guidance."

43:26–34. Joseph inquires into the brothers' "welfare," literally their "peace" (43:27). My, how things have changed since the days when they "could not speak peaceably" with him (37:4). The brothers must find it odd that after making such a big deal of their bringing Benjamin, the Egyptian official's first inquiry is not about him but about their father. And when he gets around to asking about Benjamin, he does not wait for an answer but greets him as though he already knows him (43:29). Perhaps most puzzling, the official makes no reference to the earlier charge of espionage.

Joseph's special treatment of Benjamin at dinner (43:34) probably reminds the ten brothers of their father's favoritism toward "the boy." But any resentment they might feel, any puzzle-ment at Joseph's knowledge of their birth order (43:33), and any lingering anxieties for their safety are all soon forgotten. With a full meal set before them, these ten famine victims do not have any attention to spare for their Egyptian host's baffling behavior.

44:1–13. Next morning, well-fed and well-supplied, the brothers prepare to depart. The Hebrew text literally says that "the men and their donkeys were sent away" (44:3), which suggests a warm picture of the Egyptians fondly saying good-bye to the brothers and giving their pack animals a friendly slap on the rump. Oblivious to the disaster that hangs over them, the defenseless brothers head home.

Their peace is shattered when the steward overtakes them and unleashes a devastating new accusation. As in their first confrontation with Joseph, the brothers sputter and stutter in disbelief at the seemingly preposterous charge.

Joseph's motives are debatable, but the effect of his plotting is clear enough. He has provided the brothers with a rationale for abandoning Benjamin, their father's other favorite son. The cup was found in Benjamin's sack. Even if the brothers do not believe Benjamin stole it, they cannot possibly prove his innocence. He *will* suffer whatever penalty the Egyptian official imposes. They may as well leave him to his fate. "Why," they might say to each other, "the Egyptian is presenting us with a golden opportunity to get rid of daddy's favorite without guilt!" There is even a monetary incentive. When the steward searches their bags for the cup, he passes over the money—which has mysteriously appeared there again—without a word. On the basis of yesterday's conversation (43:19–23), the brothers realize that nothing stands in the way of keeping it. They can grab the silver and go.

Nevertheless, the brothers tear their clothes as an expression of dismay (44:13; the action of their father when he was shown the evidence that Joseph was lost—37:34) and return together to Joseph's house. Disloyal to Joseph, they will now be loyal to Benjamin.

44:14–17. Again taking the lead, Judah admits to Joseph that they are guilty in some inexplicable way (44:16). He is vague about the nature of their guilt, although we as readers know exactly what it is.

In response, Joseph confronts them with a hopeless dilemma. They can save themselves and their families by returning home without Benjamin—and watch their father die with grief ("go up in peace to your father" is cruelly ironic). Or they can remain with Benjamin—without being able to help him—and their father and families will starve.

44:18–34. Judah now makes a moving appeal. He says nothing about Benjamin's innocence; that's a lost cause. But he has noticed Joseph's interest in their father (43:27), and he plays to it (mentioning "father" fourteen times). Judah proclaims his father's love for the son he lost and for the son he is about to lose—and describes the suffering his father will experience if this favored son does not return.

Years before, Judah helped to dispose of Joseph because he envied Joseph's place in their father's affections. Now he refers quite openly to his father's favoritism toward Joseph and Benjamin. Jacob has not actually said, "You know that my wife bore me two sons" (44:27). But Judah puts these words in his father's mouth to express his father's favoritism of Joseph and Benjamin—a favoritism that excludes Judah himself from his father's love. Rather than viewing this favoritism as a reason for envy and hatred, Judah now offers it to Joseph as the reason why Joseph should be merciful to Benjamin.

In a perverse way, Judah's envy of Joseph showed how greatly he desired his father's love. His conquest of this envy shows that something even more powerful than this desire is at work in him. This something is his love for his father. That Jacob will love Joseph and Benjamin more than his other sons is a fact that Judah can never change, but he has decided to accept his father as he is. Simply, Judah has determined that he will love his father even if his father does not love him. Out of love for his father, Judah is even willing to take Benjamin's place as Joseph's slave.

At the end of his pleas, Judah abandons the polite form of reference to his father ("your servant my father") and cries out in anguish: "How can I go back to my father if the boy is not with me? I fear to see the suffering that would come upon my father" (44:34). Judah remembers his father's grief at the sight of Joseph's blood-stained coat and will do whatever is necessary not to see that scene repeated. Since then, Judah has lost two sons of his own (38:7, 10). Perhaps this experience has given him an insight into his father's grief at the loss of Joseph and (as he fears) of Benjamin.

Questions for Application

40 minutes
Choose questions according to your interest and time.

1 What are the positives and the negatives in the way that Jacob and his sons handle their disagreement (42:36–43:15)? What principles are crucial for working through family conflicts successfully? What can be learned from Jacob and his sons?

2 Joseph is hard for his brothers to read. What makes it difficult to discern a person's real motives? Is it possible to grow in the ability to size people up and relate to them appropriately?

3 Alice has wronged Barb. Should Barb wait until Alice asks for forgiveness before extending forgiveness? Can Alice and Barb be reconciled if Alice does not acknowledge that she has wronged Barb?

4 How well do children understand their parents? Do children grow in their capacity to understand their parents as they themselves grow older? How do children's perceptions of their parents' weaknesses change as they grow older? What has been your experience of this, as a child or as a parent or both?

5 What kinds of experiences may help a person to grow in compassion? What impedes this growth? What could you do to grow in compassion for other people?

6 When have you willingly accepted some kind of difficulty or suffering in order to lighten the difficulty or suffering of another person? What have you learned from this experience? Where could you put that lesson to work today?

7 For personal reflection: As with last week's questions, choose one of the questions above and consider how it touches on some area in your life. What is God calling you to do in this area? Pray about this.

Do not grieve because Scripture is greater than you. The thirsty person gladly drinks, but does not grieve because he cannot deplete the spring.

St. Ephrem

Approach to Prayer

15 minutes
Use this approach—or create your own!

♦ As last week, pray the prayer below for families.

Merciful God, you have created us to live in peace, but often we do not achieve peace in our closest relationships. Shine your light in our darkness, and give us the wisdom that leads to wholeness.

Pause silently. Then take turns praying the petitions (feel free to add to the list), concluding each item as a group with "Lord, have mercy."

For family situations in which we do not understand one another and need new insight . . .

For situations in which we have been hurt and misunderstood and need to learn to trust . . .

For situations in which our patience with one another has been exhausted and our compassion needs to be renewed . . .

For situations in which we are hurt and angry and find it difficult to forgive . . .

End with an Our Father.

A Living Tradition

Not Yet "Free at Last"

This section is a supplement for individual reading.

Judah begs Joseph to take him as his slave instead of Benjamin. To most of us, the misfortune of being someone's slave is a possibility so remote as to be unthinkable. Yet the U.S. Department of State's Office to Monitor and Combat Trafficking in Persons reports that "slavery and bondage still persist in the early twenty-first century. Millions of people around the world still suffer in silence in slave-like situations of forced labor and commercial sexual exploitation from which they cannot free themselves."

Twenty-first-century slavery has many faces: a twelve-year-old girl weaving carpets in South Asia; a boy picking cocoa beans in West Africa; an abducted woman cooking and cleaning for a master in the Sudan; a young woman, tricked by an offer of employment, forced to work as a prostitute in Eastern Europe.

The U.S. Department of State estimates that 800,000 to 900,000 adults and children are taken in a condition of bondage across international borders each year. This does not count those transported within national boundaries. Human trafficking "appears to be on the rise worldwide," the office reported in 2003.

While historically many Christians were involved in the trade and ownership of slaves, the Christian tradition of resistance to slavery is also long and deep. Christian leadership in the abolitionist movement in Britain and the United States in the eighteenth and nineteenth centuries is well-known.

In medieval Europe, several religious orders sprang up with the express goal of rescuing slaves. In the thirteenth century, for example, St. Peter Nolasco, a Barcelona merchant, gave his own money to ransom Christians kidnapped by North African pirates, and he founded a group, consisting mostly of laymen, to carry on this work. In their constitution, they made this commitment: "All the brothers of this order must always be gladly disposed to give up their lives, if it is necessary, as Jesus Christ gave up his for us." Popularly called the Mercedarians, they raised money and traveled in person to ransom slaves. When the group's funds were inadequate, they would stay behind in North Africa as pledges until the full payments for released captives arrived. Inevitably, some of the group lost their lives in the process.

For more information, see page 96.

I AM YOUR BROTHER

Questions to Begin

15 minutes
Use a question or two to get warmed up for the reading.

---

1   What was the most difficult move you ever made from one home to another?

---

2   When was the last time you cried in public? How do you feel about people crying in public?

Opening the Bible

5 minutes
Read the passage aloud. Let individuals take turns reading
paragraphs.

The Reading: Genesis 45; 46:28–31

Joseph Removes His Mask

45:1 Then Joseph could no longer control himself before all those who stood by him, and he cried out, "Send everyone away from me." So no one stayed with him when Joseph made himself known to his brothers. 2 And he wept so loudly that the Egyptians heard it, and the household of Pharaoh heard it. 3 Joseph said to his brothers, "I am Joseph. Is my father still alive?" But his brothers could not answer him, so dismayed were they at his presence.

4 Then Joseph said to his brothers, "Come closer to me." And they came closer. He said, "I am your brother, Joseph, whom you sold into Egypt. 5 And now do not be distressed, or angry with yourselves, because you sold me here; for God sent me before you to preserve life. 6 For the famine has been in the land these two years; and there are five more years in which there will be neither plowing nor harvest. 7 God sent me before you to preserve for you a remnant on earth, and to keep alive for you many survivors. 8 So it was not you who sent me here, but God; he has made me a father to Pharaoh, and lord of all his house and ruler over all the land of Egypt. 9 Hurry and go up to my father and say to him, 'Thus says your son Joseph, God has made me lord of all Egypt; come down to me, do not delay. 10 You shall settle in the land of Goshen, and you shall be near me, you and your children and your children's children, as well as your flocks, your herds, and all that you have. 11 I will provide for you there—since there are five more years of famine to come—so that you and your household, and all that you have, will not come to poverty.' 12 And now your eyes and the eyes of my brother Benjamin see that it is my own mouth that speaks to you. 13 You must tell my father how greatly I am honored in Egypt, and all that you have seen. Hurry and bring my father down here."

14 Then he fell upon his brother Benjamin's neck and wept, while Benjamin wept upon his neck. 15 And he kissed all his brothers and wept upon them; and after that his brothers talked with him.

The Brothers Return to Jacob

16 When the report was heard in Pharaoh's house, "Joseph's brothers have come," Pharaoh and his servants were pleased. 17 Pharaoh said to Joseph, "Say to your brothers, 'Do this: load your animals and go back to the land of Canaan. 18 Take your father and your households and come to me, so that I may give you the best of the land of Egypt, and you may enjoy the fat of the land.' 19 You are further charged to say, 'Do this: take wagons from the land of Egypt for your little ones and for your wives, and bring your father, and come. 20 Give no thought to your possessions, for the best of all the land of Egypt is yours.'"

21 The sons of Israel did so. Joseph gave them wagons according to the instruction of Pharaoh, and he gave them provisions for the journey. 22 To each one of them he gave a set of garments; but to Benjamin he gave three hundred pieces of silver and five sets of garments. . . . 24 Then he sent his brothers on their way, and as they were leaving he said to them, "Do not quarrel along the way."

Jacob and Joseph Are Reunited

25 So they went up out of Egypt and came to their father Jacob in the land of Canaan. 26 And they told him, "Joseph is still alive! He is even ruler over all the land of Egypt." He was stunned; he could not believe them. 27 But when they told him all the words of Joseph that he had said to them, and when he saw the wagons that Joseph had sent to carry him, the spirit of their father Jacob revived. 28 Israel said, "Enough! My son Joseph is still alive. I must go and see him before I die."

46:28 Israel sent Judah ahead to Joseph to lead the way before him into Goshen. When they came to the land of Goshen, 29 Joseph made ready his chariot and went up to meet his father Israel in Goshen. He presented himself to him, fell on his neck, and wept on his neck a good while. 30 Israel said to Joseph, "I can die now, having seen for myself that you are still alive."

31 Joseph said to his brothers and to his father's household, "I will go up and tell Pharaoh, and will say to him, 'My brothers and my father's household, who were in the land of Canaan, have come to me.'"

Questions for Careful Reading

10 minutes
Choose questions according to your interest and time.

1 What does Joseph mean by his statement to the brothers: "It was not you who sent me here, but God" (45:8)? Compare 45:4.

2 Do the brothers ask Joseph's forgiveness?

3 Why don't the brothers weep when Joseph embraces them (45:14–15)?

4 Why does Joseph advise his brothers not to "quarrel" on the trip back to Canaan (45:24)? (The Hebrew word may also mean "be afraid." What might they fear?)

5 Expanding on the story, St. Ephrem wrote, "When the brothers told Jacob about Joseph, their father asked them, 'Did you not ask Joseph how or why he went down to Egypt?' Then they looked at each other and did not know what to say." What do you think they told Jacob?

6 In addition to Joseph's statement (45:5–9), where else in the story has God been secretly at work?

A Guide to the Reading

If participants have not read this section already, read it aloud. Otherwise go on to "Questions for Application."

45:1–15. Has Joseph deliberately arranged this opportunity for his brothers to demonstrate their repentance of their crime against him by showing loyalty to Benjamin? If so, he has succeeded brilliantly. Judah, presumably speaking for all, has more than passed the test. Joseph can at last reveal himself and be reconciled with his brothers.

But what if Joseph has been seeking revenge or has been wavering between harshness and love (see page 58)? In that case, Judah has not only passed Joseph's test; he has put Joseph to the test.

Recall that earlier Joseph thought God was helping him to forget his father and family (41:51). Now he declares a radically different view of what God has been doing with him: "God sent me before you to preserve life," he declares to his brothers (45:5). When did Joseph come to this new understanding of God's action in his life? Was it when his brothers first appeared in Egypt (42:6–17)? Was it three days later, when he released most of them from prison (42:18–20)? Or is it only now? Does Judah's willingness to accept slavery in place of Benjamin challenge Joseph to reconsider his own values? Does Judah's commitment to the family spur Joseph to rediscover his own commitment?

Perhaps, struck by Judah's willingness to suffer in order to preserve his father from suffering, Joseph makes a rapid review of his own past suffering and realizes that it was all part of a divine plan to relieve the sufferings of others. Perhaps, as he looks into his brother's face, full of anguish at the thought of his father's grief, Joseph is moved to accept his own kidnapping, enslavement, and imprisonment as suffering on behalf of the family.

Whenever it is that Joseph comes to see the possibility that his suffering was part of God's plan for the good of his family, he faces the decision of whether to embrace this plan or reject it. By deciding to accept this divine plan, he puts himself in a position to be reconciled with his brothers. Fundamentally, Joseph's offer of reconciliation to his brothers rests not on their repentance but on his willingness to accept his enslavement and imprisonment as having been necessary for their welfare.

Judah's appeal to Joseph has confronted him with their father's pain. For love of his father, Judah is willing to take Benjamin's place in slavery. Is Joseph now grieved at the thought of the pain *he* has caused his father by the game he has been playing with his brothers? Does compassion for his father move him to put an end to the game and be reconciled with his brothers? It seems significant that Joseph's first words on revealing himself concern not his brothers but his father: "Is my father still alive?" (45:3). Even before embracing his brothers, Joseph gives them instructions about bringing his father to Egypt (45:9–13). Joseph's longing for his father, we may suspect, has been a hidden dimension of his experience throughout the entire story. Whatever has been going on in Joseph's heart, his love for his father now draws him together with Judah. Their shared determination not to cause their father further sorrow constitutes the common ground on which they can stand together as brothers again.

Once he reveals himself, Joseph speaks quite explicitly with his brothers about their crime against him (45:4–5, 8). Reconciliation is not based on glossing over the injury they did to him.

45:16–28. Long ago the brothers brought their father evidence that Joseph had been killed; now they arrive with evidence that he is very much alive (45:25–26). God has overruled them; God's love has proven to be greater than their hatred.

Jacob's single word speaks volumes: "Enough!" (45:28). "It states his acceptance of all that has befallen him," W. Lee Humphreys writes, and "is a signal that excessive outpourings of emotion will no longer govern him." Fittingly, Judah, who played the pivotal role in making the reunion possible, acts as advance man to arrange for his father's meeting with his long-lost son (46:28).

Only Joseph weeps at their meeting. Robert Alter suggests that we imagine "a sobbing Joseph who embraces his father while the old man stands dry-eyed, perhaps even rigid, too overcome with feeling to know how to respond, or to be able to respond spontaneously, until finally he speaks, once more invoking his own death, but now with a sense of contentment: 'I may die now, after seeing your face, for you are still alive.'"

Questions for Application

1 What is the connection between having compassion for other people and being able to perceive God's plans for our own lives?

2 What is the connection between seeing God's hand in our own lives and being able to forgive those who hurt us?

3 When has acknowledging wrongdoing been crucial for repairing a relationship between you and another person? What did you learn from this experience? Is there a situation now in which you should take action in light of what you learned?

4 After the scene in 45:1–15, what further steps would Joseph and his brothers need to take to rebuild their relationship with each other? What goes into reestablishing a relationship between people after trust has been destroyed?

5 In what way is a person's desire for parents' love a permanent part of them? How may a person be affected by the frustration of this longing? How can a person's relationship with God play a part in dealing with this?

6 Have you ever gone through a hard time and realized how God was in it for your good? What have you learned from this experience?

7 Are there healthy and unhealthy ways of accepting suffering on behalf of one's family? If so, what are the criteria for making a distinction?

8 For personal reflection: When do you find it especially difficult to forgive? What resources can help you to forgive? Who do you need to forgive?

Holy Scripture is put before the eyes of our mind like a mirror in which we can view the condition of our soul.

St. Gregory the Great

Approach to Prayer

15 minutes
Use one of these approaches—or create your own!

◆ Psalm 105 celebrates God's faithfulness to the ancestors of the people of Israel as they lived in expectation of settling in the land of Canaan. Pray part of the psalm in thanksgiving to God for the hidden ways in which he is with you as you make your way with Christ to your eternal home with him. If everyone has the same translation, pray the psalm aloud together; otherwise, let participants pray aloud successive verses from their particular translations.

Specifically, pray Psalm 105, verses 1–22; then go back and pray verses 1–6 again. End with a Glory to the Father.

Saints in the Making

A Slave in Ireland

This section is a supplement for individual reading.

My father, Calpornius, a deacon, had a small country estate, where I was taken captive. At the time I was just under sixteen years of age." The speaker is St. Patrick, recalling how Irish pirates abducted him, somewhere in present-day England or Wales, around AD 400. They sold him as a slave in Ireland.

Despite his family background, Patrick declares that at the time, "I did not know the true God." But, he writes, "after I came to Ireland, then every day I tended sheep and often during the day I would pray, and more and more the love of God and fear of him came upon me, and my faith was increasing . . . because the Spirit was burning within me."

After six years, Patrick was guided through a dream to flee his master and make the dangerous trip across Ireland to the eastern coast, where he found a ship's captain willing to take him back to Britain. Some years later, Patrick had another dream. In this one, Irish people were calling to him: "Holy boy, come and walk among us again!" "I was pierced to the heart," he writes. He sought training for the priesthood and was eventually consecrated bishop. Then, despite any lingering resentment toward the people who had kidnapped and enslaved him, he returned to Ireland. Using the knowledge of the Irish language that he had gained during his captivity, he preached the gospel far and wide. Thousands of men and women came to faith in Christ.

Looking back at the end of his life, Patrick thanked God for his conversion in captivity and for the missionary work that came to him through it. He had not forgotten the suffering of enslavement. "Unwillingly I traveled to Ireland, until I almost expired," he wrote. "But this was rather for my good, because by it the Lord healed me and prepared me for what was then far from me, that is, that I should take a concern and indeed work hard for the salvation of others, whereas then I did not think even about my own. . . . I am greatly indebted to God, who showed me such kindness that so many people should be reborn into God through me."

Shades of Joseph!

Afterwords

Joseph's reconciliation with his brothers in chapter 45 is deep and moving. Yet the reader may wonder whether the relationship between them is entirely restored. The brothers are terrified. And even when Joseph calms their fears, it is he who weeps on their necks; with the exception of Benjamin, they do not weep on his. Have they repudiated all their envy of him? Will they now be able to trust that he has repudiated all thoughts of revenge toward them?

These questions receive no clear answer in the chapters that follow. The family moves to Egypt; Joseph carries out his role of provider to Egypt (in a way that increases Pharaoh's control over the people); Jacob gives his final blessing to his sons. Seventeen years pass. Jacob dies, and his family travels to Canaan to bury him there. At this point, the questions reappear. The ten brothers express to Joseph their fear of him and beg him not to punish them now that their father is no longer present (50:15–21). Apparently not all has been resolved in the grand reconciliation scene in chapter 45.

Once again, Joseph comforts his brothers with the reassurance that he is content to see God's hand in the events that divided them decades before. He has no desire for revenge. This time, the incident contains hints of closure. For the first time, the brothers ask Joseph for forgiveness. He renounces any ambition of playing God in anyone's life (is this a repudiation of the way he had manipulated them after they first came to Egypt?). This is the seventh occasion on which Joseph weeps. Often in Scripture seven symbolizes completeness. Here it suggests that Joseph has cried all the tears that are to be cried over the sufferings of the past. At last he has surmounted the sorrow of those events.

Finally, Joseph dies at the age of one hundred and ten. In Egyptian thinking, one hundred and ten years constitutes the perfect life span. In some respects, Joseph has lived the perfect Egyptian life. For an Egyptian aristocrat, the ideal life consisted of successful service in the government, army, and temple system, culminating in occupying positions of authority directly under Pharaoh. The ideal also had a strong ethical dimension: a good life included helping the poor. Thus the tombstones of countless

Egyptian aristocrats, unearthed by modern archaeologists, bear testimonies by the deceased that they held high office and earned Pharaoh's full confidence, and that they gave clothes to the naked and food to the hungry, assisted the elderly, and gave free ferry rides across the Nile to those who had no boats. Looking back on Joseph's life, one can see that he achieved both aspects of this ideal. He was entrusted with Pharaoh's full authority, and he saved the whole land from starvation. One can picture Joseph portrayed on an Egyptian tombstone, sitting in a fine chair with a table piled with good things before him, and lines of hieroglyphics all around declaring his services to king and society.

Joseph started out as a lad tending sheep in Canaan. But when, after enslavement and imprisonment, he regained his freedom, he declined to return to his homeland. He had started a new life in his new land. With God's help, he stayed and made a success of it. He served his new country well. This did not mean that he ceased to care for his family. In fact, his help became crucial to their survival. But he had become an Egyptian, and he did not go back to Canaan. Readers who have left their homeland and have begun a new life elsewhere, who have made their new land their home and have not looked back, will perhaps understand Joseph better than the rest of us.

Joseph stands somewhat apart from the continuing story of his family and people. It is not Joseph himself but his two sons—Manasseh and Ephraim—who give their names to tribes among the people of Israel. Joseph is rarely mentioned in the rest of the Old Testament.

But his role was not exhausted in Egypt. As St. Ambrose pointed out in the fourth century, Joseph stands as a foreshadowing of Jesus. In his willingness to be reconciled with his brothers, he prefigures Jesus, who forgave his enemies from the cross. In the sufferings that enabled him to preserve his brothers' lives, he prefigures Jesus, who dies to bring eternal life to all men and women.

What's the Story with Joseph's Dreams?

In the story of Joseph, four men receive message-bearing dreams. As readers, we can be confident that we learn the meaning of the dreams of the butler, the baker, and the pharaoh because Joseph interprets them and events bear out his interpretations. What about his own dreams? Joseph does not provide an interpretation of them; his brothers and father do (37:5–11). Is their interpretation correct?

Joseph's first dream, according to his brothers, means that he will rule over them. His father, Jacob, thinks the second dream predicts that even father and mother will bow down to him. It is easy to see how Joseph's family reached these conclusions. The most prominent detail in Joseph's dreams—prominent because it appears in both of them—is the act of bowing down. In the first dream, the brothers' sheaves of grain bow before Joseph's sheaf. In the second, sun, moon, and stars bow down to him. The interpretation, then, must have leapt out at his family, as it has to many readers: Joseph will rule over his family. Some modern commentators call this meaning "obvious." Joseph's dreams, they write, are so "transparent" as not to require interpretation.

But is the matter quite so simple? The other dreamers did not find their own dreams transparent. Cupbearer, baker, and king all looked for someone to unlock the meaning of their night visions (40:8; 41:8, 24). We do not know when Joseph acquired the gift of interpreting dreams, but it is possible that, in the beginning, he, too, was unable to discover the meaning of his own dreams. Perhaps he described his dreams to his family not from pride but from a desire to find out what they meant.

The manner in which Joseph's brothers and father give their interpretation raises a suspicion that they may not have quite grasped the message. While Joseph prefaces his interpretations with a declaration that insight into dreams comes from God (40:8; 41:16), his brothers and father make no such reference to God. Does their interpretation lack the necessary divine guidance?

On close examination it appears that events do not play out precisely according to the interpretations of Joseph's brothers and father. The brothers interpret Joseph's first dream to mean that he will "reign" over them (37:8). They use a Hebrew verb corresponding to the word for king. "Will you actually *be king* over us?" they demand. The answer would have to be no. Joseph never reigns over anyone. In Egypt, Pharaoh reigns; Joseph merely shares in Pharaoh's authority. Events after Joseph reveals himself to his brothers underline Joseph's subordination to Pharaoh. When Joseph instructs his brothers to bring Jacob and the rest of the family to Egypt, his instructions require Pharaoh's confirmation (45:9–20). When the brothers return to Egypt, Joseph cannot by himself settle them in the land. They must get their green card, so to speak, from Pharaoh (47:1–6), who alone has the authority to admit them as permanent immigrants and grant them pastureland.

Even more striking is the lack of fulfillment of Jacob's interpretation of Joseph's second dream. Jacob never bows down to his son. And, of course, neither does Joseph's mother, Rachel, who is already dead at the time of his dream.

The cupbearer's, baker's, and king's dreams are fulfilled precisely according to Joseph's interpretations. It seems odd that of all the dreams in the story, only those of Joseph would not be precisely fulfilled. Perhaps Joseph's dreams *were* fulfilled according to their true meaning, but that meaning eluded his family. Not that the family was entirely mistaken: Joseph did rise to a position of leadership in his family. But perhaps *dominance* over his family was not the dreams' main message.

Some scholars draw attention to the fact that the other dreams in the story refer to food and drink. The cupbearer's dream assures him that he will once more give Pharaoh his cup of wine. The baker's dream alerts him to his doom: never again will he wheel the dessert cart into Pharaoh's banquet hall. Pharaoh's dreams announce that Egypt will have good harvests followed by bad ones. Food symbolism certainly features in Joseph's first dream: Joseph and his brothers are represented by sheaves of wheat or barley. Perhaps, like the other dreams, the message of Joseph's dreams also concerns food. Rather than focus on the bowing down of the brothers' sheaves (a sign of subservience), perhaps we should focus on the height of Joseph's sheaf (a sign of his abundant supply of food). If so, perhaps the dream's message is not that Joseph will *rule* over his family but that he will *provide* for them. One very direct piece of evidence in favor of this interpretation is simply that that is exactly how things turn out.

Joseph's behavior suggests that he himself ultimately comes to this view of his dreams. Joseph never does offer an explicit interpretation of his dreams. But his interpretation is implied by the way he treats his brothers in his final recorded interaction with them. After Jacob's death and burial, the brothers send a plea to Joseph, begging him not to take revenge on them now that their father is gone (50:15–21). Joseph is so unhappy about this untrusting plea that he weeps. When his brothers arrive and bow down before him, he rejects this gesture of subservience and reminds them that God put him in a position to supply what the family needed for survival.

What, then, is the meaning of Joseph's second dream, which does not contain anything edible? One scholar, Ron Pirson, observes that the other dreams in the story contain indicators of time: three days in the cupbearer's and baker's dreams, fourteen years in the dream of Pharaoh. He suggests that Joseph's second dream provides clues to the timing of his first dream. The objects that appear in the second dream—sun, moon, and stars—are the heavenly bodies created by God as indicators of times and seasons (1:14–18). Perhaps that is their function in the dream.

What periods of time might they be indicating? Pirson suggests two possibilities. (1) One sun plus one moon plus eleven stars equals thirteen; this is the number of years until Joseph becomes second-in-command in Egypt (37:2; 41:46). (2) One sun plus one moon equals two; two times eleven stars equals twenty-two; this is the number of years that pass until Joseph is reconciled with his brothers (thirteen years until he comes to power plus seven years of abundance plus two years of famine—45:6). Both dates mark crucial stages in the fulfillment of the first dream. Here and there in the Bible there is evidence of deliberate number games on the part of the authors. Pirson's suggestion of a simple number game here seems plausible.

Thus, it seems possible that Joseph's first dream bears the message and the second the timing. The bowing, present in both dreams, serves to tie the two dreams together.

If, indeed, Joseph's dreams focus on his future role as family provider, they highlight two aspects of Joseph's experience. On the one hand, by foretelling his rise to a position of power where he will control vast resources, the dreams point to the invisible hand of God. The dreams testify to the divine sovereignty that works mysteriously through circumstances, despite the opposition of human beings, to bring Joseph to the place God had in mind for him.

On the other hand, the dreams underline Joseph's freedom. Once God put him in a position of power and his brothers came and bowed down before him, Joseph faced a choice. Would he use the position God had given him for the good of his family? Would he step into the role of provider that had been foretold of him? Whether this aspect of the dream would be fulfilled depended on him. He was free to accept or reject the invitation from God implicit in his situation—a freedom dramatized by his seeming initial indecision: at first he did not give his brothers the food they sought, but soon he changed his mind (42:14–20).

The narrator seems to provide clues that Joseph experienced an inner struggle over how to relate to his brothers. But however one reads the story—whether one sees a Merciful Joseph or a Conflicted Joseph—surely his enslavement and false imprisonment caused him great suffering. Whether at the beginning, when he first saw his brothers in Egypt, or at the end, when Judah pleaded for Benjamin's release, Joseph had to *choose* to accept both his rise to power and his suffering as gifts from God that put him in a position to care for his family.

What about us? What dream does God have for each of us? Will we trust in his power to bring it about? Will we accept our particular resources and sufferings as the God-given plan that puts us in a unique position to serve our fellow human beings?

Suggestions for Bible Discussion Groups

Like a camping trip, a Bible discussion group works best if you agree on where you're going and how you intend to get there. Many groups use their first meeting to talk over such questions. Here is a checklist of issues, with bits of advice from people who have experience in Bible discussions. (A planning discussion will go more smoothly if the leaders have thought through the following issues beforehand.)

Agree on your purpose. Are you getting together to gain wisdom and direction for your lives? to finally get acquainted with the Bible? to support one another in following Christ? to encourage those who are exploring—or reexploring—the Church? for other reasons?

Agree on attitudes. For example: "We're all beginners here." "We're here to help one another understand and respond to God's word." "We're not here to offer counseling or direction to each other." "We want to read Scripture prayerfully." What do *you* wish to emphasize? Make it explicit!

Agree on ground rules. Barbara J. Fleischer, in her useful book *Facilitating for Growth,* recommends that a group clearly state its approach to the following:

- *Preparation.* Do we agree to read the material and prepare the answers to the questions before each meeting?
- *Attendance.* What kind of priority will we give to our meetings?
- *Self-revelation.* Are we willing to help the others in the group gradually get to know us—our weaknesses as well as our strengths, our needs as well as our gifts?
- *Listening.* Will we commit ourselves to listen to one another?
- *Confidentiality.* Will we keep everything that is shared *with* the group *in* the group?
- *Discretion.* Will we refrain from sharing about the faults and sins of people who are not in the group?
- *Encouragement and support.* Will we give as well as receive?
- *Participation.* Will we give each person the time and opportunity to make a contribution?

You could probably take a pen and draw a circle around *listening* and *confidentiality.* Those two points are especially important.

The following items could be added to Fleischer's list:

♦ *Relationship with parish.* Is our group part of the adult faith-formation program? independent but operating with the express approval of the pastor? not a parish-based group?

♦ *New members.* Will we let new members join us once we have begun the six weeks of discussions?

Agree on housekeeping.

♦ *When will we meet?*

♦ *How often will we meet?* Meeting weekly or every other week is best if you can manage it. William Riley remarks, "Meetings once a month are too distant from each other for the threads of the last session not to be lost" *(The Bible Study Group: An Owner's Manual).*

♦ *How long will meetings run?*

♦ *Where will we meet?*

♦ *Is any setup needed?* Christine Dodd writes that "the problem with meeting in a place like a church hall is that it can be very soul-destroying" given the cold, impersonal feel of many church facilities. If you have to meet in a church facility, Dodd recommends doing something to make the area homey *(Making Scripture Work).*

♦ *Who will host the meetings?* Leaders and hosts are not necessarily the same people.

♦ *Will we have refreshments?* Who will provide them? Don Cousins and Judson Poling make this recommendation: "Serve refreshments if you like, but save snacks and other foods for the end of the meeting to minimize distractions" *(Leader's Guide 1).*

♦ *What about child care?* Most experienced leaders of Bible discussion groups discourage bringing infants or other children to adult Bible discussions.

Agree on leadership. You need someone to facilitate—to keep the discussion on track, to see that everyone has a chance to speak, to help the group stay on schedule. Rena Duff, editor of the newsletter *Sharing God's Word Today,* recommends having two or three people take turns leading the discussions.

It's okay if the leader is not an expert on the Bible. You have this booklet, and if questions come up that no one can answer, you can delegate a participant to do a little research between meetings. Perhaps someone on the pastoral staff of your parish could offer advice. Or help may be available from your diocesan catechetical office or a local Catholic institution of higher learning.

It's important for the leader to set an example of listening, to draw out the quieter members (and occasionally restrain the more vocal ones), to move the group on when it gets stuck, to remind the members of their agreements, and to summarize what the group is accomplishing.

Bible discussion is an opportunity to experience the fulfillment of Jesus' promise "Where two or three are gathered in my name, I am there among them" (Matthew 18:20). Put your discussion group in Jesus' hands. Pray for the guidance of the Spirit. And have a great time exploring God's word together!

Suggestions for Individuals

You can use this booklet just as well for individual study as for group discussion. While discussing the Bible with other people can be a rich experience, there are advantages to reading on your own. For example:

◆ You can focus on the points that interest you most.

◆ You can go at your own pace.

◆ You can be completely relaxed and unashamedly honest in your answers to all the questions, since you don't have to share them with anyone!

Our suggestions for using this booklet on your own are these:

◆ Don't skip the Questions to Begin. The questions can help you as an individual reader warm up to the topic of the reading.

◆ Take your time on the Questions for Careful Reading and Questions for Application. While a group will probably not have enough time to work on all the questions, you can allow yourself the time to consider all of them if you are using the booklet by yourself.

◆ After reading the Guide to the Reading, go back and reread the Scripture text before answering the Questions for Application.

◆ Take the time to look up all the parenthetical Scripture references in the introduction, the Guides to the Readings, and the other material.

◆ Since you control the pace, give yourself plenty of opportunities to reflect on the meaning of Joseph's story for you. Let your reading be an opportunity for these words to become God's words to you.

Resources

Bibles

The following editions of the Bible contain the full set of biblical
books recognized by the Catholic Church, along with a great deal
of useful explanatory material:
- ◆ The Catholic Study Bible (Oxford University Press), which
  uses the text of the New American Bible
- ◆ The Catholic Bible: Personal Study Edition (Oxford University
  Press), which also uses the text of the New American Bible
- ◆ The New Jerusalem Bible, the regular (not the reader's)
  edition (Doubleday)

Books

- ◆ W. Lee Humphreys, *Joseph and His Family: A Literary Study*
  (Columbia, S.C.: University of South Carolina Press, 1988).
- ◆ Information on slavery and trafficking in persons (p. 75) may
  be obtained from Anti-Slavery International, a British
  organization founded in 1839 (www.antislavery.org) and its
  sister organization in the United States, Free the Slaves
  (www.freetheslaves.net). Regarding the Mercedarians (the
  order still exists!), see www.orderofmercy.org. The Web site
  of the U.S. Department of State's Office to Monitor and
  Combat Trafficking in Persons is at www.state.gov/g/tip.

How has Scripture had an impact on your life? Was this booklet
helpful to you in your study of the Bible? Please send comments,
suggestions, and personal experiences to Kevin Perrotta, General
Editor, Trade Editorial Department, Loyola Press, 3441 N. Ashland
Ave., Chicago, IL 60657.